Literature of Som&
'With Compar

Wisdom is Content Out of the Knowledge

Anwar Maxamed Diiriye

Pulished by:
Gobaad Communications & Press
P. O. Box 141091, Minneapolis, Minnesota 55414.

Copyright ©2006 by Anwar Maxamed Diiriye

No part of this work may be produced or transmitted in any form or by any means, electronic or mechanical, including photocopying and recording, or by any information storage and retrieval system, without the prior written permission of its author.

All questions and inquiries should be directed to:
Gobaad Communications & Press
P. O. BOX 141091
Minneapolis, MN, 55414
United States of America

ISBN: 0-9726615-1-4
Library of Congress Catalog Number: 2005939091
Compiled, edited, printed and bound in the United States of America

Anwar Maxamed Diiriye.
Literature of Somali Onomastics and Proverbs with Comparison of Foreign Sayings / Anwar Maxamed Diiriye.

p. cm.

Includes appendixes and bibliographical references.
1. Culture—Somalia. 2. Somalia- Literature. 3. Somalia—History. 4. Somalia—Language.

I. Title.

Culture, Language, Literature, History/Africa

Pulished by:
Gobaad Communications & Press
P. O. Box 141091, Minneapolis, Minnesota 55414.

Table of Contents

Dedication -- 4

Map of Somali Inhabited Territories ---------------------------------- 5

Acknowledgements --- 6

Forward --- 7

A Note on the Spelling of Somali names ----------------------------- 9

Introduction --- 12

Chapter One
Indigenous Names --- 27

Chapter Two
Arabic or Islamic Names -- 90

Chapter Three
Somali Proverbs with English Translation ---------------------- 112

Chapter Four
Selected Non-Somali Proverbs ------------------------------------- 170

Appendixes -- 216

Abbreviations --- 226

A Note on the Author --- 227

Selected References & Bibliography --------------------------- 228

Dedication

To my beloved parents Maxamed Diirye Maxamed and Xaliima Khaliif Shiddo; my grandmother Xaliima Xasan Mataan; my aunt Khadiija Cigaal Maxamed; my uncle Cabdiraxmaan Diirye Maxamed "Bardacad" and my children Cabdulqani and Cabdulmajeed, Allah may bless them all.

This dedication is not a lip service, but it came from the bottom of my heart because each one of those dedicated to this volume touched my life directly in different times. My mother passed away when I was 18 months old and my paternal grandmother took me to her custody; my aunt Khadija, half-sister of my father was in my grandmother's household and also to mention my other uncle Cabdulaahi Cigaal Maxamed, another half-brother of my father was in the household, too. These three lovely relatives of mine made me not to feel the hardship of motherless ness and cared for me dearly during the early years of my orphaned life.

When I reached the age of five my uncle Cabdiraxmaan Diiriye Maxamed, who was a member of Somalia's police force at the time removed me from the harsh condition of the bush and nomadism, and took me to my first urban life where I started my schooling at age six and finished my secondary education at age sixteen; so, I call my high school completion age one of the luckiest of my generation. My uncle (may Allah rest him in peace) cared for me a lot and he was my sole moral and material support during that time. Unfortunately, he passed away while I was away from home and living abroad.

My children, Cabdulqani and Cabdulmajeed shaped my way of life and contributed to my happiness. I can't forget their sweet glances and their heart-warming looks and smiles; I wish for them the best of long lives with brighter and prosperous future.

Map of Somali Inhabited Territories

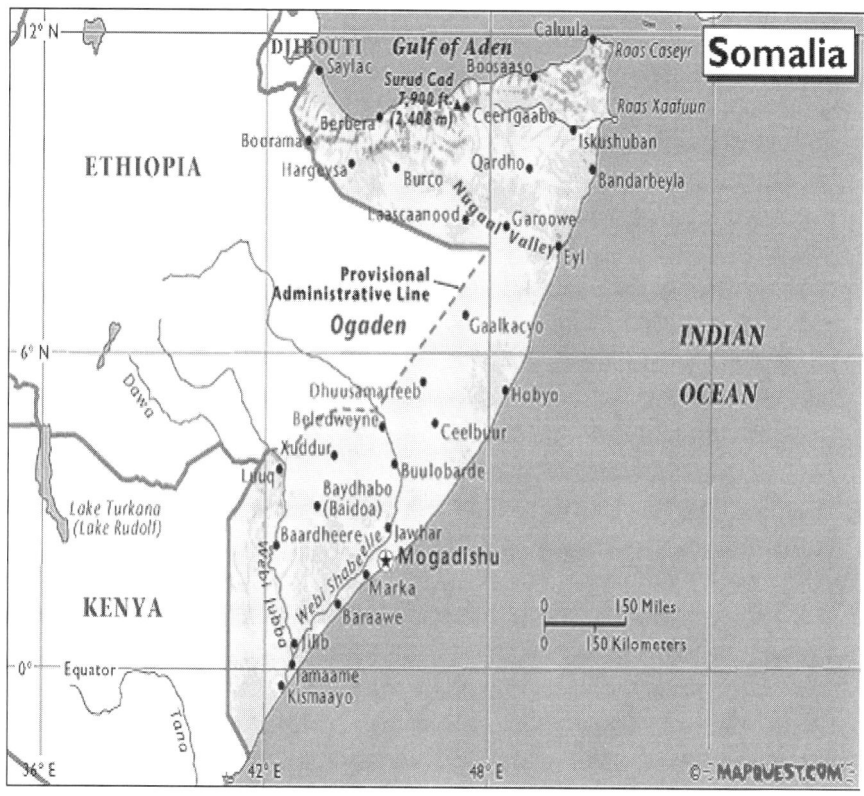

Somalis are scattered widely in the horn & eastern African territories and reside more than seven countries such as eastern Ethiopia, Djibouti, Somalia and Northeastern Kenya. They also immigrated to Tanzania, Uganda, Zambia, South Africa, Burundi, Rwanda, Republic of Congo (formerly Zaire), Zimbabwe, Botswana & Mozambique. In the Arabian Peninsula they reside inYemen, Qatar, Arab Emirates, Saudi Arabia, Bahrain and Kuwait. In North America and Europe, there are more than one million Somalis.

Acknowledgements

My thanks must go to Dr. Maxamed Daahir Afrax (Independent Somali Scholar), Mr. Aadan Diiriye Cali (Poet), Dr. Cabdisalaam Maxamed Ciise Salwe (Lacturer at Thomas Valley University of England), Dr. Cabdirashiid Maxamed Shire (Scientist at Mayo Clinic of Rochester), Mr. Idris Yuusuf Cilmi (Institute of languages in Djibouti) and Prof. Cismaan Salaad Xirsi (Geologist at the University of Regina) for all of their heartily help, corrections and dedications they gave to me during the many stages on the way to publication, and for details of formatting and production.

A special debt of gratitude must be expressed to Sacdiya-dhool Maxamed Xasan, Ubax Maxamed, Deeq Aadan Diiriye (editor-in-chief of Gobaad Cultural and Literary Journal) and Burhaan Xasan Jaamac without whose dedication and industry this volume of Somali Onomastics and Proverbs would not have achieved its production and status. Mr. Cabdiraxmaan Maxamed Warsame "Gacmo" and Siciid Axmed Warsame "Gaashaan" both assisted in computer support and the technical corrections.

I would especially like to thank Mr. Cabdullaahi Axmed of the Library of Congress, for providing much-needed materials and advice during the last stages of the book. My friend Dr. Abdi Sheik-Abdi (Academician), edited and proof-read this volume and I am very grateful for his skillful work, guidance, sincerity and corrections. Mr. Siciid M M Shire 'Suugaan" (collector of Somali materials) also deserves my gratitude for his assistance and constructive critical advice in the production of this book.

Last but not the least; I am indebted to thank Cabdirisaaq Xaaji Xuseen (former primeir of Somalia 1964-1967) and Maxamed Cabdillaahi Riiraash (Somali scholar) who read parts of this book as a manuscript of their elderly guidance and wisely advices. It goes without saying, however, that any and all residual errors are my responsibility alone.

Anwar Maxamed Diiriye
Minneapolis, Minnesota
June 22, 2006

Foreword

This Somali-English dictionary of Somali onomastics and proverbs is the result of a monumental effort on the part of the young Somali scholar, Mr. Anwar Maxamed Diiriye. It attempts to produce a reliable reference work that can serve not only the needs of any outsiders curious about Somali language and culture but also the crying needs of a new Somali generation in the diaspora who are either cut off or alienated from such culture.

The work is divided into two parts: a straight forward translation of Somali diction and a second part which attempts to illuminate traditional proverbs; the foundation of all wisdom in any preliterate society. But before we proceed any farther, a word on the long and brilliant "Introduction" is in order. This section of the work is an excellent overview of Somali and Muslim cultures. Then, there is a very lucid and highly informative discourse on the practice of naming all things in the physical and natural world; beginning with "Prophet" Adam up to the present. This is where the intriguing title of the work comes from. According to *Webster's English Dictionary*, **Onomastics** means: *the study of the origin and history of proper names*. Mr. Diiriye, citing sources, writes as follows:

A name is simply a word, phrase or sentence by which a human being is by it, he or she is identified, called, described, distinguished and classified. Nothing on earth and in much of the heavens exists without a name...A name conveys history, culture, heritage, language and a consciousness of self-image and pride. Onomastics (study of names) involves many disciplines such as history, geography, linguistics, literature, philosophy, anthropology, psychology, sociology, theology, and even the legal and medical sciences... In all, identity is the underlying feature and the principal one.

Mr. Diiriye has a nice format which allows him to first give the Somali term, then its Anglicized version or equivalent, and finally its meaning in English. For instance, Baxsan or Bahsan (Good, Nice);

Diiriye or Dirie (Comforter, Warmer); Caaggan or Aggan (Abstinent) Shacni or Sha'ni (Elegant); etc.

Now back to the spelling and proper rendering of Somali language sounds. At one point Mr. Diiriye juxtaposes the modern spelling of names in the new Latinized Somali script with their traditional Anglicized spellings. For instance, Abdulrahman is now spelt as Cabdulraxmaan; which accurately reflects the Somali language's guttural proclivities. This not only represents the guttural sounds; but also accurate vowel values.

A third part of the work is a brave attempt by Mr. Diiriye to universalize all of African and Middle Eastern cultures through this medium. He includes in this work many Arab, Berber, Bushman, Igbo, Pigmy, Swahili, Yoruba and even English sayings and proverbs. Here are some examples in Shona, they say *"One who applies proverbs gets what he wants"*; in Somali, we have *"A man with a sense of humor is never at a loss for words of action,"* in Sierra Leone, they say *"Proverbs are the daughters of experience,"* and in Yoruba, one saying goes like this: *"A wise man who knows proverbs reconciles difficulties"*.

This is not only a *toure de force* on the part of Mr. Diiriye, but a very valuable tool for all students of traditional culture. The only weakness I can note here is perhaps the ambitious nature of this work, given its limited scope. I think that one short-coming can be easily corrected.

Dr. Abdi A. Sheik-Abdi

A Note on the Spelling of Somali Names

The transcription of Somali proper names usually varies between different authors; however, it is not difficult to recognize the persons or places that are being referred to. For instance, different authors might write down the same name as Cabdulraxmaan, Abdulrahman or Abdirahman. As for Somali words, these are given as they appear in Somali Latin orthography with the pronunciation of the Somali tongue. I didn't use an anglicized version of the names. For example, the pharyngeal-voiced fricatives, noted by the letter **"c"** in the Somali orthography, is marked with a superscript **"c"** but the pronunciation of this sound can be approximated as an **"a"** by the non-native speakers of the Somali language. The pharyngeal voiceless fricative, noted by the letter **"x"** in the Somali orthography, has been written as such, but can be pronounced as an **"h"**. Additionally, the three letters **"dh," "q"** and **"kh"** are written as they are and can be pronounced as **"d," "k"** and as that found in the Scottish language sound of "loch" respectively. Here are some examples of anglicized Somali names with their meanings:

Somali	Anglicized	Meaning
Cabdulraxmaan	Abdulrahman	The servant of God
Xaydaan	Haydan	Circular fence
Cigaal	Egal	Long ranch shot
Baxnaan	Bahnan	Innate character
Cawiif	Awif	Off-white (color)
Bood	Bod	Beige-white (color)
Baxsan	Bahsan	Good, nice
Caaggan	Aggan	Abstinent
Faarax	Farah	Happiness
Cumar	Omar	Longevity
Cigalle	Egalle	Acquirer
Diiriye	Dirie	Warmer, comforter
Shacni	Sha'ni	Beauty
Qalanjo	Kalanjo	Actress
Qamar	Kamar	Moon

| Raage | Raghe | Saturn; long staying |

Here is another example of other names, which are very identical in both uses:

Somali	Anglicized	Meaning
Hira	Hira	Tall and beautiful
Sagal	Sagal	Rays of light
Samawada	Samawada	Peace maker
Samatar	Samatar	Doer of good
Milgo	Milgo	Germination
Bullo	Bullo	Olive brown
Hagar	Hagar	Insincere
Sahal	Sahal	Easiness
Abyan[1]	Abyan	Complete
Ebyan[2]	Ebyan	Complete
Gallad	Gallad	Gratitude
Barni	Barni	Date sp., tall & beauty
Libin[3]	Libin	Victory
Mahad	Mahad	Gratitude
Geri	Geri	Giraffe; taller

If the name ends the vowels of 'a or o' that means that name is feminine; if the name ends the vowel of 'e' that means that name is masculine; if the name ends the vowel of 'I' it means that name is either feminie or masculine and there are no names ending in 'u' in the Somali nomenclature system. See, the example below of gender classification by vowel sound of the Somali language.

Musculine	Meaning	Feminine	Meaning
Geyre	cold wind	Geyro	cold wind
Barkhad	very beneficial	Barkhado	very beneficial
Geri	giraffe; tall	Shacni	adorable
Abaadi	longevity	Abaada	longevity

---

[1] Masculine
[2] Feminine
[3] Unisex

Sifeeye	distinguisher	Sifeeya	distinguisher
Mahad	gratitude	Mahado	gratitude
Magadle	tanned hide	Malabo	honey; sweet
Mardaaddi	elegance	Cayni	pretty
Mako	Mecca	Soofe	grindstone
Rooble	rainmaker	Roobo	rainmaker
Geelle	rich	Geello	rich
Geeddi	caravan	Geeddiyo	caravan
Caymo[4]	be secure	Marwo	gentle lady

---

[4] That is a good example of rare exceptions!

11

Introduction

The issue of names raises perennial questions. A name is simply a word, phrase or sentence by which a human being is known. By it, he or she is identified, called, described, distinguished and classified. Nothing on earth and in much of the heavens exists without a name. There are names for people, things, buildings, trees and places, and also for storms and hurricanes. Man-made and natural phenomena alike are known through their names.

A name conveys history, culture, heritage, language and a consciousness of self-image and pride. Onomastics[5] (study of names) involves many disciplines such as history, geography, linguistics, literature, philosophy, anthropology, psychology, sociology, theology and even the legal and the medical sciences. It engages concern with character, personality, adoption, education, marriage, conversation, migration and death. In all, identity is the underlying feature and the principal one.

Personal names and nicknames provide an important component of Somali cultural identity. They reach across regional, geographical and national boundaries and extend identity from the Cushitic to the Muslim world. Somali names, like its language itself, provide their bearers with a sense of oneness in spite of its homogenous ethnicity. For Somalis, names and naming operate significantly to maintain social link and in the development of culture and individuality.

Names symbolize social organizations. They indicate ethnic and tribal affiliation, status, privilege, gender, religion and achievement within specific contexts. They transmit historical and cultural information. A name is essential in establishing connections with one's kin and community and in weighing the essence of a person or thing. The one who names an object, a place or a person often has control over the relevance of that person, place or thing. Adam (peace be upon him) was taught all the

---

[5] Encarta World English Dictionary describes it as (the study of the history and origin of proper names, especially personal names)

names so that he might have knowledge and power to use them. Every human being, male and female, is his own Adam, entrusted in his knowledge and commanded with a responsibility for the good of humanity and for all contemporary and future generations.

Chapter one deals with the indigenous names in the Somali nomenclature system and there are about 1550 of them. Somalis do not have surnames in the Western sense. To identify a Somali, three names must be used: a given name followed by the father's given name and the grandfather's. Women, therefore, do not change their names at marriage. Unlike Western societies, which have mostly separate pools for given, and family names Somalis have one pool for all three names. As a result, many names are similar and confusing to foreigners.

Perhaps for this reason, nearly all men and some women are identified by a common name *"naanays"*[6]. There are two kinds of *"naanays"*: overt nicknames, similar to Western nicknames, and covert nicknames, which are used to talk about a person but rarely used to address that person. Examples of overt nicknames are Raage (he who delayed at birth), Madoobe (very black), and, for someone who has lived abroad, Gaal (foreigner). Examples of covert nicknames are Laba-sacle (the man with only two cows) and Wiil Waal[7] (crazy boy). Famous people are sometimes referred to as "son or daughter of ". Thus the Sayyid[8] is frequently called Ina Cabdille Xasan (son of Cabdille Xasan).

Traditionally, parents chose their children's names in consultation with religious leaders, astrologers, and older family members. In recent years, however, it is more common to simply name children after a relative or a family friend without consulting anyone. Two exceptions to this tendency are first children, commonly named Faduma or Mohammed (Islamic or

---

[6] *Nin aan naynaas lahayni waa ri' gees jaban* (A man who has no nickname is like a goat with a broken horn)
[7] Ugaas Cawil Ugaas Faarax, a well-known tribal chief
[8] The leader of the Somali Dervish movement (1856-1920)

Arabic names) if you will, and male twins, commonly named Hassan and Hussein.

At the birth of a child, Somalis usually hold a feasting ceremony to welcome the newborn to the world and that is called *wal-qal* (naming ceremony). The child is given a name within the first seven days after he or she is born. The name is picked by his or her parents or sometimes by his or her relatives. According to Prophet Muhammad's Sunna (traditional teachings), in a girl's ceremony one goat or sheep is slaughtered and in a boy's ceremony two goats or sheep. Normally, parents have to follow that tradition and they have to give their child one of the best names, either from Islamic or Somali traditions.

The origin of Somali names is often either Cushitic[9] or Arabic, with the latter more common and supplanting the former. Most names have meaning, and certain names are given to denote time of birth, physical characteristics, birth order, environment, general situation, location of the birth and so on. However, it should be noted that many names are not exclusively male or female. Ideas and notions concerning the gender of names vary and change from society to society and also from one generation to another. Furthermore, it is always likely that names currently out of use may regain popularity in a later period, while new names may come into circulation. However, some names never grow old and remain favorites, such as Maxamed and Caasha as non-native examples, and Warsame and Samatar as native.

A name reflects and reinforces an identity, both when it is given and when it is changed. Thus, this book will be of special interest to parents and relatives searching for names for their newborn. In these days of mounting interest in identity and culture, this book will meet the needs of many Somali and others who may wish to know the meanings of the names they choose. From it they will learn their social and cultural significance. They will be able to select names not only on the basis of their sound, but also as reflecting their aspirations for their children and themselves. For non-Somalis, the book will contribute cultural knowledge to

---

[9] Branch of the Afro-Asiatic languages to which the Somali language belongs.

today's discourse on the values and aspirations of people of different norms and customs. The book will also be useful to anyone interested in the Somali naming system. This world is united or divided by language and nuance. It is also united and divided by its names.

Thus, Somali names are categorized with qualities; for instance as physical qualities such as Cadde (white); bellicose qualities such as Colow (combatant); social qualities such as Kulmiye (unifier); qualities pertaining to time of birth such as Jimco (Friday) or Bariise (sunrise); qualities pertaining to good auguries for the newborn such as Warsame (good news) or Macow (sweet). Also, there are names given to ward-off the evil eye, such as Xaarwaraabe (hyena droppings).Women's names are categorized differently than men's and mostly are inspired by physical or moral qualities that one desires for the newborn girls. Good examples of feminine names are Ceebla (the one without fault); Dahabo (The Golden One or Goldie); Isniino (Monday) and Qalimey (the silver one). Mostly feminine nomenclature deals with women's character, behavior, dignity, morality, beauty, season or the time of birth and so forth.

Chapter two in this book deals with the Arabic or Islamic infused names in the Somali nomenclature system and there are about 650 of them. An important source of Muslim names consists of the ninety-nine attributes of Allah[10] mentioned in the Qur'an and the *Hadith*.[11] According to Islamic belief, the relationship between man and his Creator is that of servant and master. A Muslim feels gratified and honored to be named as a servant of one of the attributes of Allah, e.g. Abdul Rahman, means Servant of the Most Gracious; or Abdul Rahim, Servant of the Most

---

[10] On the authority of Abu Huraira who said: "The Messenger of Allah said: 'Allah has ninety-nine names; whoever remembers them will enter paradise'. "Bukhari: Adab no. 2736)
[11] Sayings and practices of Muhammad (pbuh). The letters 'pbuh' in this context signifies 'Peace be upon him'

Merciful. The *Hadith* states that the best names are derived from the roots, 'thanking Allah' and 'servant of Allah'.[12]

A Muslim is pleased to discover his/her name, or a derivative of it, mentioned in the Qur'an or *Hadith*. The two well-known names of the Prophet (pbuh) mentioned in the Qur'an, Muhammad[13] and Ahmad[14], are a favorite choice for boys. However, it is accepted that part or parts of a Muslim name derive from the local language, culture or place of residence. The purpose of this chapter is to give the meaning or bearing on Islamic or Arabic heritage of the Arabic words which form parts of Somali's Muslim names.

It is important to note that the first thing that Allah taught Adam[15] was names.[16] In the Qur'an, when the wife of 'Imraan[17] gives birth to her daughter (who later became the mother of Prophet Issa[18]), she says to Allah: "I have named her Maryam"[19] (Surat Al-'Imraan 3:36). This Qur'anic verse reminds us that an important parental duty is the suitable naming of a newborn baby. In the well-known *Hadith*, Prophet Muhammad (pbuh) advised Muslims to be careful when selecting names for their children: "On the Day of Resurrection, you will be called by your names and the names of your fathers; so keep beautiful names."[20] A

---

[12] See Abd-el-Jawad, Hassan, 'A Linguistic and Socio-cultural Study of Personal Names in Jordan'. Anthropological Linguistics, XXVIII, p. 86 (1986)

[13] Honorable, praised, praiseworthy; last Prophet of Allah

[14] More, most grateful, praiseworthy

[15] Man, human being, earth; Prophet in the holy Qur'an

[16] "And he taught Adam all the names, then showed them to the angels, saying: Tell me the names of these if you are right. They said: 'Glory to you. We have no knowledge saving that which You have taight us. You, only You, are the Knower, the Wise.' He said: 'O Adam! Tell them their names.' When he had told them their names, He said: 'Did I not tell you that I know the secrets of heavens and earth? And I know that which you disclose and which you hide'."

[17] Prosperity, be long lived

[18] Biblical Jesus (Peace be upon him)

[19] Blessed, honorable, noble; biblical Mary; mother of Prophet Issa; biblical Jesus (Peace be upon him)

[20] Bukhari: Adab no. 6178

distinguishing feature of Muslim names in general is that they are inspired by the teachings of Islam in the Qur'an and *Hadith*. "Names are selected because they are religiously acceptable and are rejected because they are religiously unsound."[21] Unfortunately, many Somalis think that each name of Arabic sounding character as a Muslim name, but that is not always true. However, this chapter deals with these names as they are but does not distinguish which are Islamic and which are not.

It is very important that parents and guardians should devote enough time in selecting suitable names for their new-born boys and girls by consulting authentic books on names and re-checking them from standard Arabic-English and/or Somali-English dictionaries, if available. It should be noted that there are certain rules or patterns regarding the formation of Muslim names. Nuturally, classical Arabic names were formed in accordance with the customs of Arabia whence Islam spread. Traditionally, Arabic names prevalent in Arabia conform to the following parts or components:

(1) **Kunya** or nickname, e.g. Abu (father) or Umm (mother) of the first-born son or daughter. Prophet Muhammad (pbuh) was known as Abu Qasem, father of Qasem,[22] the name of his son. But in the Somali peninsula, this type of *kunya* is unknown while the *kunya* of 'Ina', which means 'son of or daughter of', is very common as we mentioned before. In the Arab world, it is possible that a childless person may have a *kunya*. For example, the Prophet Muhammad's (pbuh) wife Aisha,[23] although childless, was known as Umm Abdullah (mother of Abdullah[24]). Sometimes *kunya* is used in a figurative or metaphorical sense. In the non-Arab countries, one may find

---

[21] See Sheniti, Mahmud, 'Treatment of Arabic Names', International Conference on cataloguing Principles Report, 1961, p. 268.
[22] Self control, just, divider, distributor, well-tempered, cool, patient
[23] Alive, living; prosperous
[24] The Servant of Allah

only a figurative *kunya*, e.g. Abu Fadl[25], endowed with bounty.

(2) **Isim** or proper name, e.g. Muhammad.

(3) **Nasab** or lineage, son (Ibn, Bin)[26] or daughter (Bint)[27] of so-and-so. Some people are known by their *Nasab*, e.g. Ibn Rushd (1126-98), the great philosopher, known in Europe as Averroes; Ibn Batutah (1304-78), the famous traveler and explorer, known as the 'Arab Marco Polo'; Ibn Khaldun (1332-1406), the famous historian, known as 'father of historiography'. In the Somali peninsula, *Nasab* is normally used informally.

(4) **Nisba** or relationship to the place of birth, residence, descent or sometimes the name of the *Mad-hab* (school of jurisprudence) which one follows. "*Nisba*: an adjective ending *i* and proceeded by *al* indicating place of origin, descent, or membership of a tribe or sect, e.g. al-Hashimi."[28] Muhammad Ibn Ismail (810-70), the famous author of one of the *Sahih Hadith*, is known by his *nisba* al-Bukhari from his place of birth, Bukhara. Anyhow, this is not common in the case of the Somali naming system; but sometimes it's possible to see someone who is carrying his or her birthplace's name as a *naynaas* (nickname) after his or her given name such as Hawa Jirriiban, Hawa from Jirriiban district of Somalia.

---

[25] A renowned author in the Maghul court during the reign of Emperor Akbar
[26] Equivalent to Somali 'Ina' or son of '
[27] Equivalent to Somali 'Ina' or 'daughter of'
[28] See Chaplin, A.H., 'Names of Persons', National Usages for Entry in Catalogues, p. 1. "Any name can be made an attribute by adding the Arabic letter ya' in duplicate at its end... When used as a part of a person's name, the nisba usually refers to a tribe or sub-tribe, to a father or grandfather, to a country or town or village..." See Sheniti, Mahmud, 'Treatment of Arabic Names', International Conference on Cataloguing Principles Report. 1961, p. 271

(5) **Laqab** or honorific title given to a person. Many of the Prophets were known by their *laqab*, e.g. Prophet Adam as Abu Bashar (father of mankind), Prophet Ibraahim as Khalil Allah (friend of Allah), Prophet Musa as Kalim Allah (one who conversed with Allah), Prophet Muhammad as Al-Amin (the trustworthy). Khalif Abu Bakar was known as Al-Siddiiq (the truthful); while Khalif Cumar was known as Al-Faruuq (one capable of distinguishing truth from falsehood).

One may notice that in the course of time, the pattern or style of Muslim names adapted itself to local traditions or cultures as Islam spread to new countries beyond its birthplace of Arabia. Thus, the naming patterns in the Somali peninsula are quite different from the Arab countries. In some Muslim countries, e.g. Egypt, Iran, and Turkey,[29] family names are well established, but in Somalia a complete liberty in selecting names means that there is no necessary continuation of the surname from father to son.

In any culture, the naming of a person is susceptible to gender, showing significant difference in the attitude of parents when naming a boy or a girl. In general, Somali parents tend to give male children names of religious significance or those bearing qualities of manhood, courage, bravery or the condition of the birth, while female children are given names bearing on Islamic values and heritage or depicting feminine qualities such as beauty, modest, virtue or even the condition of the birth.

The title of this chapter, *"Arabic or Islamic Names,"* should not suggest that the names included are used only by Muslims. It is a common knowledge that Arab names and culture are shared by Arab Christians as well. Furthermore not all the names included in this chapter, bear strict religious significance in Islam. There are many that simply reflect qualities, e.g. bravery or virtue, which are 'universal' but at the same time associated with Muslim identity in harmony with other cultures. In a proper evaluation of Muslim names, one should keep in mind that the fact that Islamic

---

[29] See Schimmel, Annemarie, 'Some Notes on Turkish Family names', Islamic Names, p. 80.

heritage and Muslim culture transcend both Arabic language and Arab culture.

Chapter three contains 650 selective Somali proverbs taken from the collection of sayings that the author compiled 17 years ago but never published. It has been orally collected from a variety of generations between the ages of 25-85 during the years of 1985-1995. By definition proverb is a brief saying that presents a truth or a bit of useful wisdom. It is usually based on common sense or practical experience. The effect of a proverb is to make the wisdom it tells seem to be self-evident. The same proverb often occurs among several different peoples. True proverbs, however, are sayings that have been passed from generation to generation primarily by word of mouth or in written form.

Over many centuries Somali literature has offered an abundance of proverbs, fables, and riddles, songs and poetry. Unfortunately that wide ranged literature was passed from generation to generation in oral form and was not written down until recently. Some learned individuals such as Sheekh Barkhadle, Sheekh Aweys, Xaaji Cali Sheekh Cabdulraxmaan Majeerteen, Sayyid Maxamed Cabdulle Xasan and others have written and collected a good portion of Somali literature, using the Arabic alphabet but nothing has survived from their texts.

After those mentioned Mullahs a number of scholars invented their own indigenous alphabets and kept another portion of literature in their newly founded scripts. Some of those scholars included Cusmaan Yuusuf Cali Keenadiid who started inventing his *Osmania script* or *Somali script* (*Far-Soomaali*) in 1920 and completed it by 1922. His invention helped Somali independence fighters greatly; Sheekh Cabdulraxmaan Sheekh Nuur Qaadi found his *Saylici Script* in 1936 which later changed names such as *Borama script* and finally came to be known as *Gadabursi script*; and finally Xuseen Sheekh Axmed Kaddare invented his *Kaddariya script* in 1952 and later on changed its name to *Abgal script*.

Thus, this section is intended to be useful reference and help for both Somalis and non-Somalis who are interested in Somali culture, language and literature. This chapter contains over four hundred proverbs with English translations and explanations by the author.

As we know its not an easy task to successfully accomplish the intent of orally dispersed literature such as these Somali proverbs and translate them into a foreign language without tampering with the original and pure meaning of their basic intent.

Therefore, since a word-for-word translation would be impossible in this kind of text, I adopted the method of giving free translation, rendering the general meaning of words, while at the same time retaining as close as possible the spirit of the original.

Generally, when translating from one language to another, a certain degree of the spirit of the original is unavoidably lost. This is particularly so in the case of translating Somali oral literature into a foreign language such as English, mainly because of the characteristic differences between the two languages.

Over many centuries Somali people have produced an abundance of proverbs, legends, fables, riddles, superstitions, songs, poetry, stories and quotes. Only a fraction of this creative treasure has been captured in print, thereby making it unavailable to the wider world. Much of this literature remains unrecorded as it continues to be passed down orally from generation to generation. Because of the oral nature of Somali wisdom, parts of it disappear in the wind with each passing generation. *"When an elder dies,"* recognizes one Sierra Leanonian proverb, *"it is as if a whole library had burned down."* In the case of Somalia, this is absolutely true.

As we said before, Somali wisdom is abundant, so why does it remain unrecorded? Because the lack of an official script blocked its recordings. The Somali language is officially scripted and written down in 1972, although there were a number of native scripts invented by Somali scholars as we mentioned earlier.

Some genres of Somali literature are more plentiful than others. Proverbs, for instance, can be found by the thousands and some of them are included in this book. Despite their abundance, it requires some sifting to find proverbs that are pithy and at the same time easily translatable.

Somali culture attached great importance to proverbs. The ability to use proverbs effectively in speech and conversation is essential to attaining positions of leadership and respect in Somali society. Several proverbs in different sources themselves attest to the importance of this trait. *"A man with a sense of humor is never at a loss for words of action,"* indicates a Somali proverb. *"One who applies proverbs gets what he wants,"* suggests a Shona proverb of Zimbabwe. *"A wise man who knows proverbs reconciles difficulties,"* claims a Yoruba proverb in Nigeria. And in Sierra Leone it is said, *"Proverbs are the daughters of experience."*

Proverbs, by stating basic principles of folk wisdom and conduct, have become an essential and enduring part of daily speech in all societies. Very often the precepts of one culture are precepts of another, for they are an outgrowth of common experiences.

Each language has its own proverbs. The phrasing is unique and contributes to the color of the language. But whatever the phraseological turns, many proverbs convey similar meanings in different forms. For example, the Somali proverb *qofkaad barashadiisa rabto saaxiibkiisaa la bartaa "whom you want to know better, you have to know his friend"* finds an equivalent in the Spanish proverb *Dime con quien andas y te dire quien eras* "tell me whom you associate with, and I'll tell you who you are" and the English proverb *"a man is known by the company he keeps"*.

Proverbs are relatively easy for non-native speakers to learn and use. Once the concept of the proverb is understood, readers can often relate it to similar concepts, in their own languages-whereas correct, natural usage of idioms requires more practice and a better *'feel'* for the language. Each proverb in this section is presented in its most common form together with a Standard English definition where appropriate. Readers are unlikely to be troubled by this flexibility if they reflect on its presence in the proverbs of their native languages. The wordings and definitions selected for this chapter are intended to help readers achieve a basic understanding of each proverb. Both non-native and native speakers of Somali will benefit from and enjoy the wealth of linguistic and cultural information to be found in this selection of Somali proverbs.

The fourth chapter deals with 650 non-native and useful proverbs from all over the world, which are more similar to Somali proverbs. In the end of this volume are also some appendixes and bibliographical references.

However, before we go in the main theme of the book, a general discussion of the Somali nation and its people is imperative. Somalia is situated in eastern Africa and it forms the cape of the Horn of Africa. It is bordered by Kenya in the south, Ethiopia in the west, Djibouti in the northwest, Gulf of Aden in the north, and the Indian Ocean in the east. Somalia covers an area of about 638,000 square kilometers, making it slightly smaller than the State of Texas in the United States. The land is mostly flat, rising in the southern and central regions to a few hundred meters above sea level near the Ethiopian border. The higher area is along the northern coast, where mountains rise to some 2,000 meters. Somalia's long coastline-about[30] 3,300 kilometers, the longest in Africa-has been vital to its trade with the Middle East, China, India and the rest of East Africa.

Climate is the primary factor in much of Somali life. With hot, dry weather year-round, except at the higher elevations in the north, most of Somalia has a semi-arid to arid environment suitable primarily for nomadic pastoralism that more than half the population practices. Agriculture is practiced primarily in the northwest and in the inter-riverine areas in the south.

Ethnically and culturally, Somalis are the most homogeneous in Africa. The great majority of the people are ethnic Somalis who speak dialects of the same language, Somali, and who practice the same religion, Islam. There are people of Bantu descent living in farming villages in the south, and Arab enclaves in the coastal cities. A small number of Europeans, mostly Italians, lived on farms in the south before the civil war.

Historically, some Somalis claim descent from Arabian families who settled on the Somali coast a thousand or so years ago. Although there undoubtedly is an infusion of Arab culture among Somalis, historians and linguists trace the origins of the Somali

---

[30] Longest coastline in Africa

people to a much earlier time in the region; and if you read the genealogical family trees of those claiming that their ancestors are from Arabia it's so much confusing because the names (Cushitic & Arab) are mixed up, intertwined and it is too hard to proof or deny its Arabian claim of authenticity.

While scholars still debate the origins of the Somalis and the time of their entry into present-day Somalia, there is no doubt that they were in the region several hundred years before the first recorded use of their name in the early 15th century. Among ancient Egyptians, Somalia was known as the Land of Punt and was renowned for its frankincense and myrrh, which it still exports. Descriptions of the northern inhabitants of the region are found in The Periplus of the Erythrean Sea, an A.D. 60 Greek guide to sailors, and in Ptolemy's Geography, compiled between the 2nd and 5th centuries; contact with Egyptian, Phoenician, Persian, Greek and Roman trader's dates to this time. In the 10th century, Chinese merchants returned home from Somalia with giraffes, leopards, and tortoises for the imperial menagerie. By this time, Arab and Persian merchants had established towns along the coasts of the northern plains and the Indian Ocean.

By the 12th century, the ancestors of some clan families were established in their present territories. Southward movements of others, however, continued into the 19th century. When the borders of the present-day Somalia were set by the colonial powers toward end of the 19th century, large numbers of Somalis were left, and today an estimated three million or more Somalis live in eastern Ethiopia and northeastern Kenya. The existence of Somalis outside the country's national borders continues to be a source of conflict in the region.

The process of the Somali conversion to Islam in the North began very early, probably in the 11th and 12th centuries. From the 13th to 16th centuries, Somalis fought in regional wars between Christians and Muslims. In the 16th century, Somali clans participated in campaigns against Ethiopia[31], then called

---

[31] Somalia's long time arch enemy because of their religious and territorial disputes. 'Ethiopia' is a Greek word meaning the land of the burned 'black' faces

Abyssinia, led by Ahmed Ibn Ibrahim Al-Ghazi[32], who was also known as Ahmed-Gran *'The Left-handed.'*

During the period of the Scramble for Africa by the European powers, Somalia was conquered by the British, Italians and French, and by the end of the century, Somalis were living under the rule of four foreign powers: The British in the North and the Northern Frontier District of Kenya; the French in the Northwest, in what is now the Republic of Djibouti; Italians in the South and Ethiopians in the Ogaden region. A Somali poet, Faarax Nuur, had this to say about Somalia's dismemberment:

> The British, The Ethiopians, and the Italians are squabbling,
> The country is snatched and divided by whosoever is stronger.
> The country is sold piece by piece without our knowledge.
> And for me, all this is the teeth of the last day!

Toward the end of the 19th century, Somalia took part in a general Muslim reaction in North Africa against colonialism. In 1899, Maxamed Cabdulle Xasan, Called the "Mad Mullah"[33] by the British and known as "the Sayyid"[34] by Somalis, launched a 20-year insurrection against colonial occupation. The Sayyid's abilities as a poet and orator, highly valued skills among Somalis, won him many disciples, and much of his success was in commanding trans-clan loyalty. Although ultimately he failed to maintain unity, the Sayyid is nonetheless viewed as one of the definers of Somali national identity.

Finally, British Somaliland and Italian Somalia achieved their respective independences on June 26th and July 1st, 1960, and elected to unite and form a unitary state to be called the Somali Republic. The former French Somaliland (now Republic of Djibouti) gained its independence on June 27th, 1977 and became a sovereign entity. On October 15th, 1969, the second president of

---

[32] Historians believe that he was of a Turkish descent, but Somalis see him as their savior hero and the military government of General Barre built a monument in Muqdisho for him

[33] British colonial officer's view

[34] In Somalis' own eyes, he was either inspired and blessed or he was a destructive devil amongst them

the new and embryonic republic, Dr. Cabdirashiid Cali Sharmaake, was assassinated and a military officer took command of the headless state. General Maxamed Siyaad Barre and his Junta declared themselves the supreme authority in the country and ran a dictatorship state until their own overthrow in 1991. Now, after 15 harsh and horrible years of anarchy and civil war, Somalia formed its first inclusive government under a former military officer, Colonel Cabdullaahi Yuusuf Axmed, who has been elected to lead in the first five years of the transition by the transitional federal parliament in Nairobi, Kenya.

õõõ

Chapter I
Indigenous Names

*Monday's child is lucky and will succeed in life with ease;
Tuesday's child is stubborn and may be exposed to injury;
Wednesday's child is unlikely to gain anything more than mediocrity;
Thursday's child is friendly and nice;
Friday's child is stubborn, strong, and combative;
Saturday's child is unlucky and vengeful; and
Sunday's child is generous*

*A myth of Aja-fon people in southern Benin
1001 African Names: First and Last Names from the African Continent
By Julia Stewart
P. 23, 24*

A

Aar *nickname; name-m* adult male lion; revenge, vengeance. Lit: very brave man
Aare *nickname; name-m* revenger; he who revenges; braver
Aawe *name-m* reason, sake. Cf: Aawo
Aayow *name-m* future, destiny; benefit from
Abaadi *name-m* longevity; long life
Abasguul *name-m* see-off the water caravan. Lit: he who is born when the water caravan starts its journey to the well during the night
Abayle *nickname; name-m* weaned (child abandoned by his mother; baby that has been weaned)
Abbow *name-m* brother
Abgaal *name-m* camel's descent, lit: he who his ancestor owns many camels
Abiib *name-m* father of the reliable one. Syn: Abuubakar

Abkaal *name-m* lineage helper
Ablaawe *name-m* of unknown descent; without ancestors; a person of unknown descent or family
Abokor[35] *name-m* father of the reliable one. Syn: Abuubakar. Cf: Abuukar, Abuubakar
Abow *name-m* brother
Abraar *name-m* stampede, rush; act of rushing. Lit: he who was born too quickly after the initial labor
Absame *name-m* noble, aristocracy, high caste person, the free born; good lineage; belongs to a good lineage, genealogy. Cf: Nasab Syn: Gobaad
Abshir[36] *name-m* good news; congratulations; the better of two ideas
Abshiro *name-f* good news; congratulations; the better of two ideas
Absuge *name-m* lineage corrector
Abtidoon *name-m* uncle-seeker; esp. the maternal uncle. Lit: he who born while his maternal uncle is present
Abtisame *name-m* one with a nice maternal uncle
Abti-udug *name-m* aromatic uncle
Abturaale *name-m* from kindly descent; kindful; merciful
Abuukar[37] *name-m* father of the reliable one. Syn: Abuubakar. Cf: Abokor, Abuubakar
Abyan *name-m* complete; done; be whole, wholesome; surprise, amazement. Syn: Ebyan, Ebyoon, Dhamme, Dhammo
Addoonwaaq *name-unisex* God's servant—or slave
Adeer *name-m* uncle
Afbalaar *nickname-m* big-mouth
Afgaab *nickname-m* quiet and polite
Afguduud *nickname-m* red-lipped
Afkudeeble *nickname-m* evil-worded
Af-qallooc[38] *nickname-m* the wry mouth

---

[35] Axmed Cali **Abokor** (scholar and author who wrote extensively about the Somali literature & culture)
[36] Gen. Maxamed **Abshir** Muuse (first commissioner of Somalia's police forces, 1958-1969)
[37] Sahra **Abuukar** 'Dawo' (singer)
[38] Xaaji Aadan **Af-qallooc** (long lived poet)

Afrax[39] *name*-m success, gain; lit: succeed, be successful
Afraxo *name-f* success, gain; lit: succeed, be successful
Afrika *name-f* Africa. Lit: black or dark skinned
Afweyne *nickname-m* mighty-mouth
Agoon *nickname; name-m* orphan
Ajuuraan *nickname-m* fee; renter; landlord
Aleemow *nickname-m* Joker
Allaale[40] *name-m* belonging to Allah. Cf: Rabbiile
Allamagan *name-m* under God's protection, sanctuary or refuge
Amarre *name-m* blessed; authorized; endowed with divine blessing; possessing supernatural power. Syn: Amran
Amartiwaaq *name-m* superiority; superior power. Lit: result of sky God's superiority
Amaan *name-unisex* trust; praised, admired. cf: Ammaanle
Ambiyo *name-m* prophecy
Ammaan *name-unisex* secure, peaceful, safekeeping.
Ammaanle *name-m* praised, admired. Syn: Ammaan
Ammaanreer *name-m* family's admiration, praiseworthy; favorite
Amran *name-f* blessed; authorized; endowed with divine blessing; possessing supernatural power. Syn: Amarre
Arab *name-m* deserts and waste barren land; well-night waterless and treeless; in Somalis' view it means a light-skinned one. He who born in a barren land or in the desert (Arb). Cf: Carab, Carabo
Aragsan *name-f* beautiful
Ararsame *name-m* articulated; nice introductory
Ardo *name-f* courtyard. Lit: she who was born in the courtyard
Arliyo *name-f* lander
Arwaax *name-f* exhilaration, happiness, thrills
Ashkir *name-m* extremely light-skinned
Ashkiro *name-f* extremely light-skinned
Asiili *name-f* genuine, pure, dignified, noble. Cf: Asli, Gobey,

---

[39] Maxamed Daahir **Afrax** & Maxamed Maxamuud **Afrax** (well-known novelist, critic, playwright, journalist and literary scholar who writes in Somali, English and Arabic , and a well-known journalist and author respectively)
[40] Cabdinuur **Allaale** (well-known Djiboutian singer & lyricist)

Sharaf

Askar *name-f* soldier. Syn: Askaro

Askaro *name-f* soldier. Syn: Askar

Asli *name-f* original; origin; pure, typical, genuine, dignified, noble. Cf: Asli, Gobey, Sharaf

Astur *name-f* preserve, cover, conceal. Lit: she who preserves, covers or conceals shame or disgrace; always positive and optimistic

Atoor *name-m* male dikdik (antelope). Lit: he who born while a dikdik is running around or is born on uninhabited dikdik environs

Aw[41] *nickname-m* a learned man of God; sheikh or mullah (prefix of title)

Awaare *name-m* dust; dust raiser. Lit: he who is born in dusty environs or is born while wind is raising dust

Awal *name-m* expectation, guesses, prediction; or it might be from Arabic as 'first', which means first-born baby

Awdaan *name-m* secured; shut, closed, covered

Awdoon *name-m* Mullah-Seeker. Syn: Sheekhdoon

Awle *name-m* yelper; yeller

Awley *name-f* yelper; yeller

Awr *name; nickname-m* stud-camel; bigger; larger

Awrtable *nickname-m* inventor of camel tethers

Awsame *nickname-m* nice Mullah

Axado *name-f* Sunday; she who was born on a Sunday

Axmed-deeq *name-m* honorable and generous

Ayaan *name-f* luck, fate, good fortune. Syn: Cawo, Nasiib, Naruuro

Ayaanle *name-m* luck, fate, good fortune. Syn: Cawaale

Aaye *name-m* destiny, future

B

---

[41] **Aw**-Jaamac Cumar Ciise & **Aw**-Muuse Ismaaciil Samatar (well-versed historian who authored many books about Somali history & dervish poetry) & a legendary poet respectively

Baadicadde *name-m* undisputed, proofed; brand, mark, insignia
Baahila' *name-f* hungerless; needless; demandless. Lit: self-sufficient
Baalcad *name-m* white-sided; lit: bald on one side of the head at birth
Baalle *nickname, name-m* winged, feathered; blessed or divined
Baar *nickname; name-f* tip, peak; lit: high caste. Syn: Baarre
Baargaal *nickname-m* tall, high caste, superior, noble
Baarleeli *nickname-m* elegance, finery, splendor; refinement, pride
Baarleex *nickname-m* he who his hair is parted
Baarliin *name-f* lime colored eyelashes; she whom her eyelashes are lime-colored at birth
Baarqab *nickname-m* spoiler; stud; lit: very arrogant, logger-headed and troublesome
Baarre *nickname; name-m* tip, peak; lit: high caste. Syn: Baar
Baaruud *nickname-m* gunpowder; pulver. Lit: warmonger
Baashan *name-f* Queen
Baashane *name-m* King
Baashi *name-m* King
Baayir *nickname-m* liar
Bacadle[42] *nickname-m* vendor, seller; dune, sandhill. Lit: he who was born at or near sandhill; or he who became a vendor/seller after he grew up
Bagaag[43] *nickname-m* bravos
Bahdoon *name-m* relative seeker; born away from home
Bahlaawe *name-m* the one who misses his clan
Barakow *name-m* blessed; divine favor
Bardacad *nickname-m* light-skinned, handsome
Bareera *name-f* intention; frankness
Barkad *name-m* he who rests on another; lit: he who born after his twin
Bariido *name-f* greeting, salutation. Syn: Bariise
Bariise *name-m* greeting, salutation. Syn: Bariido
Barkhad *name-m* very beneficial; proliferation; re-birth. Syn: Barkhadle, Barkhado

---

[42] Abshir Nuux Faarax "**Bacadle**" (poet)
[43] Cabdulqaadir Yuusuf **Bagaag** (well-known singer)

Barkhadle *name-m* very beneficial; proliferation; re-birth. Syn: Barkhad, Barkhado

Barkhado *name-f* very beneficial; proliferation; re-birth. Cf: Barkhadle

Barni *name-f* date sp. (fruit) considered the best species; lit: very light-skinned. Cf: Suuri

Barre[44] *nickname-m, name-m* specked, speckled, spotted, marked, stained. Lit: he who was born with a birth mark. Syn: Barrow, Barrey,

Barrey *nickname-f, name-f* specked, speckled, spotted, marked, stained. Lit: she who was born with a birth mark. Syn: Barre, Barrow,

Barrow *nickname-m, name-m* specked, speckled, spotted, marked, stained. Lit: he who was born with a birth mark. Syn: Barre, Barrey

Barsame[45] *nickname; name-m* he whom his settlement is safe and nice

Bartire *nickname-m* conqueror; lit: the warrior who conquers every thing on his way when he defeats his enemies

Barwaaq *name-m* sky God's niche or mark

Barwaaqo *name-m* good fortune, prosperity; lit: he who was born at a time of plenty. Syn: Sareedo Cf: Tigaad

Bashaash *nickname-m, name-m* outgoing, sociable, cheerful

Bashka[46] *name-m* the sound breaking thing makes—like the sound of the maternal water breaking. Cf: Jug

Basra *name-f* town of Basra; bright, sweetness. Lit: sweet like dates

Baxar *nickname; name-m* clever, active (Arb)

Baxnaan[47] *name-m* innate character, one's nature

Baxsan *name-f* good, nice, bright (Arb)

Baxsane *name-m* good, nice, bright

Baynax *nickname; name-m* very light-skinned, blond

Beddel *nickname-m* exchange, substitution, substitute, alternative,

---

[44] General Maxamed Siyaad **Barre** (iron fisted military ruler of Somalia 1969-1990 who lived between 1919-1995 and died in Kanu, Nigeria)
[45] Sheekh Xasan **Barsame** (well-known mullah and freedom fighter)
[46] **Bashka** Jug Soo-dhacay (BBC London's Somali Section correspondent In Garrisa, Kenya)
[47] Samatar **Baxnaan** (well-known poet)

replacement; on behalf of; instead of. Cf: Cawil
Beegsan *name-f* well-proportioned
Beerlula *name-f* liver-shaker; lit: sultry beauty
Beydan *name-f* grayer. Syn: Beyle
Beyle *nickname; name-m* grayer. Syn: Beydan
Biciido *name-f* oryx (African antelope)
Biciidyahan *nickname-m* hunter; skilled
Bicir *nickname-m* shorter and small-framed; sedentary person
Bidaar *nickname-m* bolded. Cf: Hiiraale
Bidde[48] *nickname-m* servant or slave. Lit: faithful, obedient
Biddewaaq *name-m* sky God's servant
Biinle *nickname; name-m* pinned
Biixi[49] *nickname-m* the one with the long shin-bone
Bilcil *nickname; name-m* he who born near the large thorny tree used medicinally; medicine man; herbalist
Biladdaya *name-f* mirror; telescope. Cf: Muraayad
Bilaw *name-m* beginning, start. Lit: first born son, the elder (sometimes written as Billaw). Syn: Bilow
Billaawe *nickname-m* dagger. Lit: warrior
Billan *name-f* promoter; beautiful; improvement. Syn: Bille
Bille[50] *name-m* promoter; beautiful; improvement. Syn: Billan
Bilow *name-m* beginning, start. Lit: first born son, the elder (sometimes written as Billow). Syn: Bilaw
Binin *name-m* small; tiny
Binti[51] *name-f* daughter (Arb)
Birboore *nickname; name-m* blacksmith, ironsmith
Birmad *name-f* rescuer, emergency
Bishaaro *name-f* good news; congratulations (Arb)
Bitiqo *name-f* beautiful; elegant
Biyamaal *nickname; name-m* wealth, riches, finance, prosperous, fortunate; good omen
Bogaad *name-f* appreciation, admiration, enjoyment, pleasure

---

[48] Axmed Suleymaan **Bidde** (playwright & poet)
[49] Maryan **Biixi** (poet)
[50] Cabdi **Bille** Cabdi (1500M runner who won the gold medal in 1988 Olympics)
[51] **Binti** Cumar Gacal (well-known singer)

Bogsiiya *name-f* healer
Bood *nickname-m* beige ~ white (color)
Boos *nickname-m* a decrepit person
Boosh *nickname-m* white; light-skinned
Boosteeya *name-f* female ostrich; beautiful and easy going; overshadow
Bootaan *name-m* dust; a dusty place. Lit: he who was born at a dusty place or white-skinned
Boqoro *name-f* crowned, princess. Syn: Boqran, Boqorre
Boqorre *name-m* crowned. Syn: Boqoro, Boqran
Boqran *name-f* crown prince/princess. Syn: Boqoro, Boqran
Boore *name-m* dusty colored
Budle *nickname-m* club, cudgel; lit: he who is in the habit of carrying a club
Budul *nickname-m* powder; dust. Lit: dust colored
Bulbul *nickname-m* mane; untidy hair; fluency
Bullaale *nickname-m* light skinned. Cf: Bullo, Bullow
Bullo *name-f* olive brown, Isabella color; light skinned. Cf: Bullaale, Bullow
Bullow *name-m* light skinned. Cf: Bullaale, Bullo
Bulxan[52] *name-m* talkative; the one who talks cheerfully
Bunney *nickname; name-f* coffee. Lit: black
Bunnow *nickname; name-m* coffee. Lit: black
Buraale *name-m* granular. Lit: he who is born with warts, tumors and abnormal granules on his body parts
Burgal *nickname-m* tactful; clever
Burhaan *name-m* power from God, divine favor leading to success. Syn: Burhaano
Burhaano *name-f* power from God, divine favor leading to success. Syn: Burhaan
Busur *name-f* unripe dates; lit: one born before her due date
Butaaco *name-f* gushes, out-pouring; lit: she who was born too Quickly after the first episode of labor
Buto *name-f* small plant with edible roots; lit: she who was born with too much baby fat
Buubow *nickname; name-m* runner, chaser; rejecter

---

[52] Qamaan **Bulxan** (well-known legandary poet)

Buulalle *nickname-m* anthill; lit: one who is afflicted with a skin
  Disease or pustules; hence the nickname
Buulle *nickname-m* hut owner, nestler; lit: hut owner or he who
  lives in a nest
Buuni *nickname; name-m* scholar, sage (especially in religion)
Buur *nickname-m* fattie
Buux *name-m* fullness, the state of being full. Syn: Buuxo
Buuxo *name-f* fullness, the state of being full. Syn: Buux

C

Caabbi *name-m* protect, guard by force; be capable of defense;
  support, strengthen, reinforce
Caabbiya *name-f* protect, guard by force; be capable of defense;
  support, strengthen, reinforce
Caabudwaaq *nickname; name-m* sky God's worshiper
Caafi *name-m* curer, healer
Caafiya *name-f* curer, healer
Caaggan *name-f* abstainer, abstention; lit: she who restrains from
  doing bad things, modest. Cf: Caaggane
Caaggane *name-m* abastainer, abstention. Lit: he who restrains
  From doing bad things. Cf: Caaggan
Caalami *nickname-m* international (Arb)
Caalin *name-m* learned (Arb)
Caanood *name-f* white; milkie
Caaqdoor *name-m; nickname* intelligent, wise, smart; chief,
  headman, elder, boss, king; clever, mindful
Caaqib *name-m* usefulness, goodness; fate, destiny. Syn: Caaqibo
Caaqibo *name-f* usefulness, goodness; fate, destiny. Syn: Caaqib
Caaqil *name-m* intelligent, wise, smart
Caarif[53] *name-m* expert, knowledgeable (Arb)
Caarre *nickname-m* active, vigorous
Caasila *name-f* obedient, faithful, loyal
Caateeye *name-m* cause to become skinny; cause to lose weight

---

[53] Cali **Caarif** Burhaan (former premier of Djibouti during the colonial era)

Caato *nickname-m* thin, slim, skinny
Cabaade *name-m* cry out, yeller, screamer, screecher, squealer, yelper. Cf: Ujaajeen, Wacwacle
Cabban *name-f* well-armed, ready for combat; shapely, a well-proportioned woman. Cf: Cabbane
Cabbane *name-m* well-armed, ready for combat; a well-built man; shapely . Cf: Cabban
Cabdidaahir *name-m* ritually purified servant
Cabdideeq *name-m* servant of the Generous
Cabdihodan *name-m* servant of the Rich
Cabdiyo *name-f* servant
Cabsiiye *nickname-m* he who frightens, scares, intimidator, endangerer
Cadaawe *nickname-m* enemy, cruel
Cadar *name-f* perfume, scent, aromatic; shadow. Cf: Udgoon, Dalays
Cadarre *name-m* perfume, scent, aromatic; shadow. Syn: Cadar
Cadceed *name-m* sun; daylight; sun-rays. Syn: Qorrax, Gabbal
Caddaan *name-m* white; clear
Caddaani *name-m* whitish; cearly
Caddaawe *nickname-m* whitish; light-skinned
Caddey *name-f* white, clear, clarified, proven. Syn: Caddow
Caddo *name-f* moony night; full moon
Caddow *name-m* white; be clear, clarified, proven. Syn: Caddey
Cadduur *name-m* wild tree (sp)
Cajabo *name-f* astonished, miracle, amazement, wonder, marvel
Calas *nickname; name-m* slightly light-skinned. Syn: Calaso
Calaso *nickname-f* slightly light-skinned. Syn. Calas
Calasow *nickname; name-m* slightly light skinned. Syn: Calas
Calidaahir *name-m* exalted and ritually purified
Calinuur *name-m* shined and exalted
Caliyow *name-m* exalted, high, lofty. Cf: Cali
Calwiya *name-f* made muddy
Cambaro *name-f* amber; precious
Camey[54] *nickname-m* the one with the swollen or defective cheek
Cammuud *name-unisex* sand (color)

---

[54] Xaaji Cumar **Camey** (legendary poet)

Canab *name-f* grape, vine; lit: sweet, beautiful
Carab *nickname; name-m* deserts and wastelands; waterless and treeless. It could also mean the light-skinned one (Arb). Cf: Arab
Carays[55] *nickname; name-m* taunter
Carfi *name-f* to put perfume on; be aromatic. Cf: Carfoon, Udgoon
Carfoon *name-f* fragnant; aromatic; scent. Syn: Udgoon
Caroog *name-m* trumpet
Carraale *name-m* clean; newness; freshness; challanger
Carraaba *name-f* travel in the afternoon
Carrabey *nickname-m* lisper, stammerer, stutterer
Carraweelo *nickname; name-f* conqueror; Somali legendary Queen
Carre *nickname; name-m* Sandy; challenger, darer, warner; Provocateur; agitator
Carro *nickname; name-f* Sandy; challenger, darer, warner
Cartan *nickname; name-m* anger; roarer; boiling. Syn: Carte
Cartama *name-f* anger; roarer; boiling
Carte *nickname; name-m* anger; roar; boiling. Syn: Cartan
Carwo *name-f* exhibition, fair; display
Casaro *name-f* late afternoon; afternoon prayer; lit: she who is born at late afternoon during the afternoon prayer time. Syn: Casayr
Casayr *name-m f* late afternoon; afternoon prayer. Lit: he who was born at during the afternoon prayer time. Syn: Casaro
Casey *name-f* off-red (color)
Casharo *name-m* Koranic lesson; holy water
Cashuur *nickname; name-m* tax, customs duty
Catir *name-m* black. Syn: Cidaad
Cawaale[56] *name-m* luck, fate, good fortune. Syn: Ayaanle, Cawo
Cawareere *name-m* dusk; large shark (sp)
Caweys *name-f* nighttime socialization; evening
Cawil *name-m* substitute; black. Cf: Beddel

---

[55] **Carays** Ciise Kaarshe (well-known and artful poet)
[56] Maxamed **Cawaale** Liibaan & Cali Mire **Cawaale** (two prominent figures in Somali history. Inventor of the Somali flag & the composer of the Somali national anthem song 'Wake up Somalis known as **Soomaaliyeey Toosoo**' respectively)

Cawilo *name-f* substitute; black
Cawiif *nickname-m* off-white (color)
Cawireere *name-m* good luck; good fortune
Cawke *nickname-m* the one with the protruding Adam's apple.
    Cf: Cuuke
Cawl *name-m* yellow; tan; antelope
Cawlyahan *nickname-m* expert antelope hunter; hunter, skilled
Cawo *name-f* night; luck, fate, good fortune. Syn: Ayaan, Nasiib
Cawrala' *name-f* honorable; the one without blemish; beautiful.
    Syn: Ceebla
Cawramale *name-m* shameless, honorable, noble
Caydiid *name-m* curse refuter, drool resistant
Caymo *name-m* takes refuge, be secure, be save; remainder; safety,
    Security
Caymow *name-m* takes refuge, be secure, be save; remainder;
    safety, security
Caynaanshe[57] *name-m* rescuer, savior; leader
Caynab *name-m* black. Cf: Caynabo
Caynabo *name-f* black. Cf: Caynab
Cayni *name-f* pretty; adorable; beautiful
Cayr *nickname-m* poor, starved. Cf: Xubeer
Ceebla' *name-f* honorable; without shame; beautiful. Syn: Cawrala
Ceegaag *name-m, nickname-m* rich, solid
Ceelaabe *name-m* back from the well. Lit: he who was born while
    the water caravan was coming back home
Celi *name-m* prevent, halt and stop
Cibaar *name-m* novelty, strange
Cidaad *name-m* black
Cigaal[58] *name-m* headband, turban; long range shot
Cigaalo *name-f* headband, turban; long range shot
Cigalle *name-m* acquires; take sides, substitute, substitution,
    alternative. Cf: Cige, Cubtan

---

[57] General **Caynaanshe** (one of the first victims of the military government of Somalia; killed by public shooting with Gen. Salaad Gabayre & Col. Dheel in 1972)
[58] Maxamed Xaaji Ibraahim **Cigaal** & Axmed Cali **Cigaal** (third prime minister of the Somali Republic and a well-known singer, lyricist & musician who sometimes even wrote songs, respectively)

Cige[59] *name-m* acquirer
Ciqwaaq *name-m* sky God's sound
Cirfe *nickname-m* short person. Cf: Jagfe
Ciid *name-m; nickname* holiday, religious holiday, celebration-festival, feast; soil, sand. Lit: light-skinned or; he who was born during a holiday or festival
Ciido *name-f; nickname* holiday, religious holiday, celebrate, festival, feast; soil, sand. Lit: light-skinned or; she who was born during a holiday or festival
Ciidagale nick*name-m* reptile; sand borer; sand diver; sandie
Ciilmoog *name-f* untouched by anger, peaceful of mind, innocent
Ciilmooge *name-m* untouched by anger, of peaceful nature
Ciil-tira *name-f* eraser of anger; soother, vindicator
Ciiraale *nickname-m* grayish in color; cloudish
Ciiro *name-m; nickname* gray; spotted color pattern on black; cloudy, foggy; misty. Cf: Ciire
Ciire *name-m; nickname* gray; spotted color pattern on black; cloudy, foggy; misty. Cf: Ciiro
Cillal *name-m* hidden, secret, mysterious; a plant sp. with edible tubers
Cilmi[60] *name-m* science, knowledge, education; lit: sacred, holy, divine
Cimilo *name-f* climate
Ciya *name-f* cryer. Syn: Ciye
Ciye *name-m* cryer. syn: Ciya
Ciyow *nickname; name-m* bird sp.; immediately; right away. Lit: bird that serenades or some one who born immediately after the initial labor without complications. Cf: Shimbir
Codweyn *name-unisex* the one with the great voice
Codweyne *name-m* the one with the great voice
Colaad *name-m* aggressor; fighter, warrior; hostile, hostility, enmity, antagonism. Syn: Colley
Colhaye *name-m* enemy stopper; protector
Colley *name-f* aggressor; fighter, warrior; hostility, enmity, antagonism. Syn: Colaad

---

[59] Khadra Daahir **Cige** & Saynab **Cige** (well-known singers)
[60] **Cilmi** Ismaaciil 'Boodhari' (leged love victim in the Somali folktale)

Colow *name-m* combatant, aggressor; fighter, warrior; hostility, enmity, antagonism. Syn: Colaad
Cosob *name-f* fresh, new. Syn: Cosobo, Cosoble
Cosoble *name-m* fresh, new. Cf: Cosob, Cosobo
Cosobo *name-f* fresh, new. Syn: Cosob, Cosoble
Cubtan *name-f* acquires; take sides, drawing lots. Cf: Cigale, Cige
Cudbi *name-f* cotton; lit: white, light-skinned
Cuddoon *name-f* even, propotionate, parallel, equal; well-shaped
Cugan *name-f* cleaned
Culan *name-f* pure; good hearted one
Culimmo *name-f* religious, scholar; scientist, expert
Culus *name-unisex* heavy, serious
Culusow *nickname; name-m* heavy; serious
Curad *name-unisex* first born, elder son or daughter
Cureeji *name-f* silken material; lit: precious & honorable
Cuti *nickname; name-m* elegance, finery, splendor; refinement, pride
Cutiya *nickname; name-f* elegance, finery, splendor; refinement, pride
Cuuke *nickname-m* one with a protruded Adams apple. Cf: Cawke

D

Daacad *name-m* frankness, honesty; sincerity, good nature; faithful
Daad *nickname; name-m* flood. Lit: born quickly or unexpectedly. Cf: Butaaco
Daado *nickname; name-f* flood. Lit: born quickly or unexpectedly
Daaha *name-f* late, not on time, tardy. Lit: she who was born over-due
Daahir[61] *name-m* ritual purity; religious manifestation; appearance; cleansed, ritually purified
Daahsan *name-f* late, not on time, tardy. Lit: she who was born over-due
Daanweyne *nickname-m* the one with a protruded jaw

---

[61] **Daahir** Xaaji Cismaan Sharmaarke 'Dhegaweyne' (one of the living members of the founders of the Somali Youth League).

Daar[62] *nickname; name-m* igniter; ignite, instigate
Daarood[63] *nickname-m* stone-house enclosure; mason
Daawaale *name-m* medicine man
Daawad *name-f* worth watching
Daa'uus *nickname; name-f* peacock
Dabar *name-m* hopple robe; fetter, manacle
Dabarre *nickname-m* hobbled, tethered, tied up, fettered, chained
Dable *nickname; name-m* private soldier who carries firearms; constable
Dabran *name-f* hoppled; fetted; chained
Dabshid *nickname; name-m* bonfire; Somali New Year festival (around early August). Lit: troublemaker; born during the New Year's festival; or he who was born when his family feasted with prosperity after a long, lean period; the first born son after a number of female siblings before him and his parents were longing for a son. Syn: Neyruus. Cf: Diiriye and Diirshe
Dacar *nickname; name-m* bitter
Dage *nickname-m* deceiver, cheater, ambusher
Dagoodi *name-m* dark in color or black
Dafle *nickname-m* snatcher; taker of things forcibly
Dahab *name-m* gold; golden boy
Dahabo *name-f* Goldie; golden girl
Dahsoon *name-f* covered, curtained, hidden, secret. Lit: hidden from the evil eye
Dakeeya *nickname; name-f* lie down and rest with pleasure; peaceful and prosperous. Lit: she who rests and enjoys her life without calamities
Dallaayad *name-f* shade; umbrella. Syn. Dallaayo
Dallaayo *name-f* shade; umbrella. Syn. Dallaayad
Dalab *nickname-m* knock-knee
Dalal *name-m* moans, groan. Syn: Talal
Dallays[64] *name-f* shade; she who shades or provides cover—as

---

[62] Aaden Cabdulle Cismaan **Daar** (first president of the Somali Republic, 1964-1967)
[63] One of the main Somali clan-confederacies

from the sun
Dalmar *name-m* world-traveler; explorer
Dalwaaq *name-m* God's country
Damal *name-m* acacia tree sp., Lit: born under an acacia tree.
Dangal *name-m* minder
Dangalo *name-f* minder
Darandoodle *name-m* tough; strong; orator
Darar *name-m* prosperer (born during the good pasture season)
Dararamle[65] *nickname-m* drummer; professional, traditional dancer
Darbaal *nickname-m* canvas, tarp
Darmaan *name-unisex* colt, filly, foal
Darwiish *name-m* dervish; inspired soldier
Daruur *name-m* cloud, mist
Daruuro *name-f* cloud, mist
Daryeel *name-unisex* help; caring, concerned; safeguard, preserve, nurture
Dashiishe *nickname-m* prosperous
Dawlo *name-*f state, government
Dawo *name-f* medicine, remedy
Dawsar *nickname*-m vagabond, bum, good-for-nothing, irresponsible, a lazybones; one who behaves irresponsibly
Dayax *name-m* moon. Syn: Dayaxo
Dayaxa *name-f* moon. Syn: Dayax
Dayib *name-m* good, pure, sinless (Arb). Tree type species in Somali. Lit: born near or under a Dayib tree. Cf: Dayib (in chapter two)
Daymare *nickname-m* evader; backbiter
Daynab *name-m* dark, black
Daynabo *name-f* dark, black
Deeq *name-m* donation; gift; offer; grant; generosity. Syn: Deeqa, Deeqsan
Deeqa *name-f* donation; gift; offer; grant; generosity. Syn: Deeq, Deeqsan

---

[64] Khadiijo Cabdullaahi Camey **Dalays** (first female public singer in Somali theatrical stage, performed in 1952 at Radio Mogadisho)
[65] Axmed Xaaji Cali Haaruun **Dararamle** (legendary singer)

Deeqsan *name-f* donation; gift; offering; grant; generosity. Syn: Deeq, Deeqa

Deer *nickname; name-m* light-skinned

Deerow *nickname; name-m* light-skinned

Degaan *name-m* settlement, community, habitable place, residence, a place suitable for human habitation; the act of settling

Deggan *nickname; name-f* settled, inhabited; relaxed, calm, meek, gentle, modest

Degmo *name-f* settelement; camp

Dejiya *nickname; name-f* accommodator, locator. Lit: good woman

Deyl *name-m* black

Dhaadsan *name-f* tied up; noticed

Dhaashan *name-f* creamed, greased, lubricated; well-groomed

Dhaashane *name-m* creamed, greased, lubricated; well-groomed

Dhaayo *name-f* eyes; vision; sight; enlightenment, knowledge

Dhacarbe *nickname-m* he who grazes his livestock on good pasture

Dhakal *nickname; name-m a* milking vessel. Lit: a small-framed person

Dhakool *nickname-m* isolated. cf: Gooni

Dhalac *nickname-m* heat; sun. Lit: born out of the sun heat

Dhamac *nickname; name-m* hot; charcoal, embers; torch

Dhamme *name-m* finished; complete; full; done. Syn: Abyan

Dhammo *name-f* full; done, complete; finished. Syn: Ebyan, Ebyoon

Dhaqane *nickname; name-m* cleansed; pure, sinless or well – preserved

Dharaar *name-m* day light

Dhebi *name-f* a majestic tree sp. lit: tall and beautiful or one born under that tree sp.

Dheeg *name-m* a highly elevated shop deck

Dheeggan *name-f* imitation; impersonator

Dheeha *name-f* coated, enamelled, plated

Dheel[66] *name-m* dew; amuser, joker, entertainer

---

[66] Colonel Cabdulqaadir **Dheel** (one of the first victims of the military government of Somalia; killed by public shooting with Gen. Caynaanshe & Gen. Salaad Gabayre in 1972)

Dheemman *name-f* diamond
Dheere[67] *nickname; name-m* tall-man; taller
Dheged *nickname; name-m* sticky, stickiness
Dhegtaar *nickname; name-m* extra ear; one with a small birth tumor above the ear
Dhenged *nickname; name-m* switch, a long thin stick
Dhergan *name-f* sated, full; satisfied
Dherganow *name-m* sated, full; satisfied; faithful
Dhiblaawe *name-m* easy-going; harmless
Dhicis *name-m* premature (born before his due date)
Dhicisow *name-m* premature (born before his due date)
Dhiidhi *nickname; name-m* annoyance
Dhiif *nickname; name-m* attentive, alert, active, vivacious
Dhiig *name-m* blood
Dhiimo *name-f* a deep red color; lit: beautiful with a bright light-skin. Syn: Dhiin, Maadhiin
Dhiin *name-m* a deep red color; lit: beautiful with a brighter light-skin. Syn: Dhiimo, Maadhiin
Dhiirran *name-f* brave, fearless
Dhiirrane *name-m* brave, fearless
Dhikil *name-m* small, short and weak
Dhikilo *name-f* small, short and weak
Dhilan *name-f* peeled, husked; pretty, beautiful (tall and slender)
Dhilane *name-m* peeled, husked; handsomeness (tall and slender)
Dhimbil *nickname; name-m* flash; spark; live ember(s)
Dhimbilo *name-f* flash; spark; live ember(s)
Dhimman *name-f* premature; born before her due date
Dhinbiil *nickname; name-m* flash; spark; live ember(s)
Dhiqle[68] *name-m* temperamental; lit: a high tempered one
Dhoodaan[69] *nickname-m* bragging, boasting. Syn: Shooli
Dhooddi *name-m* land with hard soil; lit: he who was born in a

---

[67] **Dheere** Xaaji **Dheere** (one of the thirteen founders of the Somali Youth League)
[68] Cabdullaahi Macallin **Dhoodaan** (well-known poet)
[69] Xuseen **Dhiqle** (the Dervish soldier and memorizer of Sayid Maxamed Cabdille Xasan's oral poems)

land with hard soil. Cf: Jeylaani, Jilani
Dhoof *name-m* travel abroad, emigrate; embark, ride off -- away; depart, leave
Dhoofo *name-f* travel abroad, emigrate; embark, ride off -- away; depart, leave
Dhool *name-f* vibration; front tooth; front of a passing rain, quick passing rain. Syn: Saylaan
Dhoorre[70] *nickname; name-m* crested bird sp.; one with the Mohawk haircut. Lit: he who was born while that bird was around or he who is in the habit getting a Mohawk haircut
Dhowre nickname; *name-m* expecting, anticipating, awaiting; protect, care giver
Dhooye nickname; *name-m* intelligent
Dhoyla *nickname-f* stupid, unintelligent
Dhudi *name-f* string; thread. Lit: proportional; Small-framed; hence beautiful. Cf: Ximyar
Dhulbahante *nickname-m* land conqueror; Mightier
Dhulqas *nickname-m* spoiler
Dhunkaal nickname; *name-m* poison, venom; troublesome or he who annoys his kin's enemy at birth
Dhuuban *nickname-f* slender and proportionate
Dhuubo nickname; *name-f* tall and slender
Dhuubow nickname; *nickname-m* tall and thin
Dhuule[71] *nickname-m* he who dresses in a leather a garment
Dhuunkaal *nickname; name-m* poison, venom. Lit: very bad; inhuman
Dhuutiyo *name-f* beautiful; elegant. Cf: Bitiqo
Dhuux[72] *nickname; name-f/m* bone marrow. Lit: pure, beautiful, handsome; obedient, loyal
Dhuxul *name-m* charcoal; black
Dhuxulow *name-m* charcoal; black
Digaale *name-m* good fortune, good luck. Syn: Falxad, Falxado
Dige[73] *name-m* alerter; warner or alarmer; lucky

---

[70] Abshir **Dhoorre** Xasan (one of Dervish's energetic commanders)
[71] Cumar **Dhuule** Cali (well-known & golden-voiced singer, lyricist and song writer)
[72] Cali Aadan '**Dhuux**' (well-known poet and Dervish freedom fighter)

Digil *name-m* arterial; jugular; important
Dihin *name-f* untouched, uncultivated; virgin and fertile
Diiddan *name-f* refused, rejected, vetoed, opposed
Diihaal *nickname-m* destitution; weakness, exhaustion
Diimmoon *name-f* newly discovered, invented; previously unknown, new
Diini *name-m* religious. Syn: Diinle
Diinle *name-m* religious. Syn: Diini
Diintiwaaq *name-m* God's faith
Diirato *nickname-m* peeler, skinner, stripper. Lit: warrior
Diiriya *name-f* warmer, comforter
Diiriye *name-m* warmer, comforter. Syn: Diirshe
Diirran *name-f* warm, tepid; intimate, close. Syn: Diirrane
Diirrane *name-m* warm, tepid; intimate, close. Syn: Diirran
Diirshe *name-m* warmer, comforter. Syn: Diiriye
Dir *name-m* origin; race; ancestor
Diraac *name-m* dry season; autumn (born during that season)
Diraaco *name-f* dry season; autumn (born during that season)
Dirir *name-m* name of a very bright star. Lit: he who has been hoped to be bright
Doobiro *name-f* luck, fate. Syn: Ayaan
Doode *name-m* orator, debator, one who debates
Dool *name-m* distant destination; strayer; stranger, foreigner, migrant
Doolaal *nickname; name-m* trespasser, interferer. Lit: the one born in a foreign land or he who always trespasses to foreign lands to rob or look for green pastures for his livestock
Doonbiro *name-f* plant sp., with edible fruit. Lit: plump, prosperous. Syn: Barwaaqo, Sareedo
Doorwaaq *name-unisex* sky God's choice
Dooyo *name-m* attacker; warrior; invader
Dooyow *nickname; name--m* attacker; warrior; invader
Dub *name-m* skin; peeling
Dubbad *nickname; name-m* hammerer
Dubbeys *nickname; name-m* hammerer; forging
Ducaale *name-m* blessed, holy man

---

[73] Cabdi Xasan **Dige** (well-known singer & lyricist)

Duco *name-f* prayer, invocation of God; blessing (Arb)
Duda *name-f* scatter, disperse (out of fear); pessimist
Dude *nickname-m* sulker; scatterer, disperser; pessimist
Dudub *name-m* strong; powerful
Duduble *name-m* mascular; strong; powerful
Dugsiiya *name-f* sheltered, weather-tight
Dugsiiye *name-m* sheltered, weather-tight
Dugsoon *name-f* weather-tight, weatherproof; sheltered
Dugul *name-m* dark, black
Dugulo *name-f* dark, black
Dulman *name-f* wronged, oppressed
Dulmar *nickname; name-f* to pass over, above all, indirect, insinuation; conveyed by implication
Duniyo *name-f* worldly; lit: very beautiful and very gentle
Durqun *nickname-m* mumbled, murmured; antagonistic, misunderstanding -- hostility within a family
Durraan *name-m* to pray or call upon (a saint); to pray to a saint, usually with gifts of money or a feast by the one who prays. Lit: he who was born after a religious man read the Qur'an over his mother
Duufaan *nickname-m* typhoon
Duullane *name-m* war-monger; attacker or slaughterer

E

Ebyan *name-f* done; complete; finished; full. Syn: Abyan, Ebyoon, Dhamme, Dhammo
Ebyoon *name-f* finished; complete; full; done. Syn: Abyan, Ebyan, Dhamme, Dhammo
Eenow *name-m* Aadan or Adam; man, human being; earth
Ereg *name-m* foster; entrust
Eymow *name-m* hunter; skilled

F

Faacuul *nickname-m* a short, chubby person

Faahiye *name-m* explainer, describer, detailer; distributor, spreader
Faarax *name-m* happiness, joyful; to be happy; joyous. Syn: Faaraxad, Farax
Faaraxad *name-f* happiness, joyful; to be happy or joyous. Syn: Faarax, Farax
Facaye *name-m* good, great, clever. Cf: Fariid, Gaawiido
Fadal *name-m* foot-print
Fagaase *nickname; name-m* bridle or bridler
Fadfadle *nickname-m* one who has pock- marks on the face
Falaqdoor *name-m* nice and merciful; very kind
Falaxfalax *nickname; name-m* an incense-bearing tree sp., a happy-go-lucky or talkative person
Fallaax *nickname; name-m* cheerful, good-natured person
Fallis *name-f* to outbid, outbidding; outscoring
Falxad *name-m* good fortune, good luck. Syn: Digaale, Falxado
Falxado *name-f* good fortune, good luck. Syn: Digaale, Falxad
Fanax *nickname-m* gap-tooth
Faqi *nickname-unisex* he/she who consults secretly
Farax *name-f* happiness, joyful; to be happy, joyous. Syn: Faarax, Faaraxad
Fariid *nickname; name-m* good, great, clever. Cf: Facaye, Gaawiido
Fariido *nickname; name-f* good, great, clever
Farxad *name-m* happiness, luck
Farxado *name-f* happiness, luck
Farxaan *name-m* cheerful, happy, merry man
Farxiyo *name-f* joy. Syn: Fayaan
Fatxi *name-m* opener of fortune. Syn: Fatxiya (Arb)
Fatxiya *name-f* opener of fortune. Syn: Fatxi (Arb)
Fayaan *name-m* joy. Syn: Farxiya
Feeyig *nickname; name-m* alert, cautious, careful
Feeyiga *nickname; name-f* alert, cautious, careful
Feynuus[74] *nickname; name-f* lamp, gas light, lantern
Fidaar *nickname-m* tall and thin
Fijiray *nickname-m* slow-mover; sluggish
Fiin *name-m* predicter; a buzzard bird sp., whose cry is believed to

---

[74] **Feynuus** Sheekh Daahir (one of the Somali female folklore dancers)

predict future events. Lit: he who was born while a buzzard bird was sitting ontop his family's hut
Fikir *name-unisex* think (Arb)
Filad *name-unisex* expectation, hope
Filsan *name-f* beautiful, good-looking—said of girls
Fiqi *nickname; name-m* whisper; he who talks secretly; religious
Fiqidoor *nickname; name-m* an exalted whisperer; exalted religious man
Firin *name-m* thin. Lit: a Somali comb made of one stick only and very common in Djibouti
Fiido *name-f* twilight, early evening. Lit: she who was born at early evening
Fiidow *name-m* twilight, early evening; lit: he who was born at early evening
Foogan *nickname; name-f* busy; raised, lifted; erected
Foogane *nickname; name-m* busy; raised, lifted; erected
Foohaar *nickname-m* sharp-dresser; elegant
Foojig *nickname; name-m* alert, cautious, careful
Foojiga *nickname; name-f* alert, cautious, careful
Foos *name-f* front line, forefront; force, armed forces
Furqaan *name-unisex* religion (Islamic faith or its book); holy one

G

Gaaceed *name-m* repulser; he who resists an invasion
Gaaceedo *name-f* repulser; she who resists an invasion
Gaaci *name-f* repulses; resist an invasion; spill
Gaaciro *nickname-m* invasion; resistance; repulse
Gaaciye *name-m* repulser; he who resists an invasion
Gaadaco *nickname-m* broad-chested
Gaadsan *nickname; name-f* the state of being ready for action. Lit: she who is always alert
Gaafan *nickname; name-f* ready, prepared, willing, predisposed. Syn: Gaafane, Gaafow
Gaafane[75] *nickname; name-m* ready, prepared, willing,

---

[75] **Gaafane** (very artistic Djiboutian comedian)

predisposed. Syn: Gaafan, Gaafow
Gaafow *nickname; name-m* ready, prepared, willing, predisposed. Syn: Gaafan, Gaafane
Gaalgale *nickname-m* infidel invader; camel looter
Gaaljecel *nickname-m* camel lover
Gaarax *nickname-m* a short man with a broad chest
Gaarhaye *nickname; name-m* sentry
Gaarri *nickname; name-f* good housewife, good woman
Gaarriye[76] *nickname; name-m* a clever man, good man
Gaarriyo *nickname; name-f* good housewife, good woman
Gaanni *nickname-m* a full-grown crocodile or a young male lion
Gaas *nickname-m* gas; paraffin, kerosene; lit: a warrior
Gaashaan[77] *nickname; name-m* shield, defense. Cf: Harti
Gaashireedle *name-m* spot, circular mark
Gaasira *name-f* diminished, reduced, born before her due date
Gaasira *name-f* diminisher, reducer
Gaatax *nickname-m* a short man with a broad chest
Gaawiido *nickname-m* good, great, clever. Cf: Facaye, Fariid
Gaaxnuug *nickname-m* sucker of the milk tank
Gabaddano *name-m* cold, chill. Lit: born in a time of a cold spell
Gabanow *nickname-m* young; lit: younger, baby
Gabar *name-m* defraud, pay in part
Gabayre[78] *name-m* a cold place; lit: born at a cold place or time
Gabal *name-m* piece; small; part
Gabbal *name-m* sun; daylight; sun-rays; spot, circular mark as a birthmark. Syn: Cadceed, Qorrax
Gaboose *nickname; name-m* dark, black
Gabyow *nickname-m* poet; verse reciter
Gacal[79] *name-m* beloved person, a dear one; darling, friend. Syn: Gacaliye
Gacaliso *nickname; name-f* beloved; dear

---

[76] Maxamed Xashi Dhamac **Gaariye** (well-known poet, literary scholar and educator)
[77] Axmadey Abuukar **Gaashaan** (singer)
[78] General Saalad **Gabyre** (one of the first victims of the military government of Somalia; killed by public shooting with Gen. Caynaanshe & Col. Dheel in 1972)
[79] Maxamed **Gacal** Xaayow (well-known poet)

Gacaliye *name-m* beloved person, dear one. Syn: Gacal
Gacayte[80] *nickname-m* small-framed and weak—said of men
Gaceed *name-m* short
Gaceedo *name-f* short and petite
Gadiid *nickname; name-m* midday; noontime shadow (when shadows are smallest); barren, infertile land (born on barren land)
Gadiido *nickname; name-f* midday; noontime shadow (when shadows are smallest); barren, infertile land (born on barren land)
Gaduudane *nickname-m* reddish, brownish or reddish-brown
Gafaaje *nickname-m* big and strong
Gahayr[81] *name-m* unripe
Galaal *nickname; name-m* whitewash, bald
Galab *name-m* afternoon, evening; lit: he who was born in the afternoon
Galabo *name-f* afternoon, evening; lit: he who was born in the afternoon
Gal-Allah *name-m* God's sheath
Galan *name-m* windy ~ showery weather
Galangal *name-m* roller, windy ~ showery weather
Galayax[82] *nickname-m* an untidy person
Galayr *name-m* eagle; lit: he who was born while an eagle was hovering overhead
Galbeyte *nickname-m* he who moves away permanently; head home after day's work
Gallad *name-m* favor, gratitude
Gallado *name-f* favor, gratitude
Galmaax *name-m* prosperous; diver; swimmer
Galool *nickname; name-m* curve, wrap; acacia tree specie
Galti *nickname-m* foreigner; from the interior; new comer
Gama'diid *name-m* sleepless; insomniac; alert
Gamas *nickname-m* small spear. Lit: warrior
Gamuun *nickname; name-m* arrow; fast

---

[80] Axmed **Gacayte** (legendary singer)
[81] Cabdi **Gahayr** (poet)
[82] Cabdi Magan **Galayax** (a heavyweight poet)

Gamuure *nickname-m* bluntness
Gammuute *nickname; name-m* bluntness
Gandaal *name-m* hide of a dead calf (used to induce the mother to give milk)
Garaad[83] *name-m* understanding, judgement, wisdom; mind, sense, thought, intelligence; chief, leader (title of leadership & respect)
Garas *name-m* a shade-tree sp., with edible fruit; lit: he who was born under that shade-tree
Gareen *nickname; name-m* hammerhead shark
Gargaar *name-m* helper; generous
Gargaara *name-f* helper; generous
Gargaarte *name-m* he who helps by himself; self sufficient
Gariirre *nickname; name-m* the one who shakes, trembles, or shivers
Garoon *name-m* field, ground, range; play field; pitch. Lit: he who born on such a field
Garre *name-m* ocean fish sp., plaintiff, lawsuit, verdict; justice, the law
Gar-xajis *name-m* lawyer; impartial arbiter; just
Gasabi *name-m* achiever
Geedde *name-m* treesome
Geeddi[84] *name-m* traveler; caravan; migration, traveling (on a journey) Lit: he who was born during a trans-humance
Geeddiyo *name-f* traveler; caravan; migration, traveling (on a journey) Lit: he who was born during a trans-humance
Geeddo *name-f* treesome
Geedow *name-m* he who born an area full of trees
Geelle[85] *name-m* camel-owner; lucky; rich. Syn: Geello
Geello *name-f* camel-owner; lucky; rich. Syn: Geelle
Geelwalaal *name-m* camel lover
Geenyo *name-f* mare, female horse; lit: one named after a female

---

[83] **Garaad** Maxamuud Cali Shire (Grand-Sultan of British Somaliland Protectorate)
[84] Cismaan **Geeddi** Raage (one of the thirteen founders of the Somali Youth League); Cali Maxamed **Geeddi** (prime minister of the transitional federal government of Somalia)
[85] Ismaaciil Cumar **Geelle** (President of the Republic of Djibouti)

horse--which is so precious in Somali culture
Geesaguulle *nickname; name-m* victory bearer
Geesood *name-m* horned. Lit: he who was born with lumps on his forehead
Gefla' *name-f* trouble less; errorless; straightforward; righteous
Geftin *nickname; name-m* edge, corner
Gendel *nickname-m* tall and curved
Geledi *name-m* insertion; inserter
Gendershe *nickname-m* he who brings people together or unites. Cf: Shiriye
Geni *name-f* Geni, guinea; pound (Sterling); twenty shillings
Geri *name-m* giraffe; tall. Lit: he who was born in environs inhabited by giraffes
Geyfan *nickname-f* the state of being ready for action. Lit: he who is always alert
Geyfane *nickname-m* the state of being ready for action. Lit: he who is always alert
Geyllan *nickname; name-m* rage, mad, fighting; strive, he who tried hard
Geyllama *nickname; name-f* rage, mad, fighting; strive, he who tried hard
Geyre *nickname; name-m* cold wind coming from the sea. Lit: he who was born while such wind is blowing; *nickname:* anger, rage. Lit: temperamental man. Syn: Geyro
Geyro *name-f* cold wind blowing from the sea; lit: she who was born while such a wind was blowing; *nickname* anger, rage; Lit: temperamental woman. Syn: Geyre
Gidir *name-m* dark, black
Gobaad *name-f* noble, aristocracy, high caste, free-born. Syn: Absame
Gobey *name-f* high caste. Cf: Gobaad, Samaale, Shuun
Gobdoon *name-m* noble or nobility seeker
Godane *nickname-m* curved, bent, arched; stooped one. Cf: Tooxow
Good *name-m* poisonous snake, copperhead
Goodir *nickname-m* as strong as male kudu (entalope); one with a dark gray color
Goolnuug *nickname-m* fattened sucker, baby fat-- said of nursing

young animals
Gooni[86] *nickname-m* isolated; difference, separateness; different, particular, distinct, peculiar; on one's own, alone. Lit: very sensitive to his own; self-centered. Cf: Dhakool
Gordan *nickname; name-f* mottled
Gorgor *name-m* vulture
Gorod *name-m* black-maned
Gorodo *name-f* black-maned
Gudaal *name-m* night traveler
Gudcur *nickname; name-m* darkness, dark, the state of being without light. Lit: black by nickname or born in a dark place by name
Guddoonwaaq *name-m* sky sky God's verdict, sky God's decision, God's resolution
Gu'dhalad *name-f* lucky; she who born during the rainy season of spring
Guduud *nickname; name-m* reddish in color; golden cat
Guduudane *nickname-m* reddish in color; golden cat
Guduudo[87] *nickname-f* reddish
Gufaaco *name-f* strong wind that brings raind and storms; born easily and faster without difficulties
Gugundhabe *nickname-m* dragon-slayer
Guhaad *name-m* anger, resentment
Guhaado *name-f* anger, resentment
Gulaal *name-m* person with hesitance-- stammering speech; male camel which is unable to control the gland in his mouth
Gumaas *nickname-m* clean cut, smooth and short
Gumansoor *nickname-m* outcaste feeder or host; merciful, kind
Gurey *nickname-m* left-handed
Gurraase *name-m* spring dwelling; the cape of spring; blessed
Gurxan *name-m* growl, roar; the act of roaring
Guud *name-m* high caste, noble; above all. Cf: Gob
Guudow *nickname-m* one with expansive mane; full head of hair,

---

[86] Xaaji **Gooni** (riddlistic poet who was the prime critic of Sayid Maxamed's literature)
[87] Shamis Abuukar '**Guduudo** Carwo' (second female public singer in Somali theatrical history, Radio Hargeysa, 1953)

free-flowing hairstyle
Guulane *name-m* victorious
Guule *name-m* giver of victory; God (pagan name)
Guuleed *name-m* victor; victorious
Guuleedo *name-f* victor; victorious
Guure *name-m* night traveler; lit: he who was born during a night time travel. Syn: Guureeye
Guureeye *name-m* night traveler; lit: he who was born during a night time travel. Syn: Guure
Guutaale *name-m* leader of armies; squad, brigade; mature. Lit: he who was born while some warriors of his kinsmen were in attendance

H

Habarwaa *name-m* he who misses his mother. Lit: he who his mother died after his birth because of birthing difficulties
Habarwalaal *name-m* obedient; kindful; merciful
Habban *name-f* right, correct, suitable, nice. Syn: Habbane. Cf: Habboon
Habbane *name-m* right, correct, suitable, nice. Syn: Habban. Cf: Habboon
Habboon *name-f* suitable, appropriate, correct, rightful. Cf: Habban, Habbane
Hadambari *name-m* blessed and clever (in Galla language)
Hadi *name-m* insence-bearing tree sp., balsam
Hadiye *name-m* healer
Hadiyo *name-f* gift
Hadraawi[88] *nickname-m* talkative, orator (Arb)
Hagar *nickname-m* insincerity, negligence, neglect of one's responsibility; refusal of help when it is needed; hesitation, denial; intentional wrongdoer
Hagarla *name-f* one who tries her utmost or who makes every effort; great effort, sincerity, negligenceless

---
[88] Maxamed Ibraahim Warsame **'Hadraawi'** (one of the leading & living Somali poets)

Halaag *nickname-m* destruction, annihilation
Halac *nickname; name-m* greedy, person with a very large appetite; large spear (warrior); hot wind ~ air; flame (tempremental)
Halakeeya *name-f* severe harm, damage, grievous wound (difficult delivery condition); or she may serve you right
Halakeeye *name-m* severe harm, damage, grievous wound (difficult delivery condition); or he may serve you right
Halako *nickname-unisex* severe harm, damage, grievous wound (difficult delivery condition); or he may serve you right
Haldhaa[89] *name-f* male ostrich. Lit: very beautiful
Hamtade *name-m* conqueror; Mightier
Hanad *name-m* able person; leader, superior
Hannaan *name-f* appearance, shape; attitude, form, style, method, system, process
Hanuuniye[90] *nickname-m* orientates, adviser, counselor, guide; spiritual director (one who guides ~ directs from a religious, political ~ theatrical point of view)
Haqabtira *name-f* satisfier, appeaser, provider
Haqabtire *name-m* satisfier, appeaser, provider
Hariin *name-m* shading, put ~ carry into the shade
Harti *nickname; name-m* sheild; man. Cf: Gaashaan
Haweeya *name-f* desire, state of desiring or overcome with desire; Lit: the elevated one
Hawiye *name-m* sweetener; to air something out; open something to let air in or out
Hayaan *name-m* long journey, hard trek, migration. Lit: he who was born during a long journey
Haybe *name-m* prestige, respect, social prominence; having a pleasing personality
Hayin *nickname; name-m* docile; simple, uncomplicated; tamed ~ trained pack camel
Hayimo *nickname; name-f* docile; simple, uncomplicated; tamed ~ trained pack camel
Heego *name-f* the gathering of clouds before rain; rainbow
Heellaale *nickname; name-m* loyal, obedient

---

[89] Faadumo **Haldhaa** (sweet-voiced Somali singer)
[90] Cabdulle Yuusuf **Hannuuniye** (Somali singer)

Heellan *name-f* loyal, obedient
Heellane *name-m* loyal, obedient
Hibo[91] *name-f* gift, present, thing bequeathed; talent, natural gift
Hidaaya *name-f* gift (Arb)
Hiddo *name-f* tradition, heritage
Hiiraale *nickname-m* bald. Syn: Bidaar
Hillaac *name-unisex* lightening, flash of lightening; flash
Hillaaca *name-f* lightning, flash of lightning; flash
Hindisa *name-f* invention, plan
Hindiyo *name-f* Indian. Lit: light-skinned
Hiirad *name-m* early morning, first light at dawn; lit: born at early morning; trouble, difficult. Lit: born with difficulty, difficult birth
Hira *name-f* tall and beautiful
Hiraab *name-m* second half of the night, from midnight until dawn. Lit: born during the second half of the night. Syn: Hiraabe, Hiraabey
Hiraabe *name-m* second half of the night, from midnight till dawn. Lit: born during the second half of the night. Syn: Hiraab, Hiraabey
Hiraabey *name-m* second half of the night, from midnight till Dawn. Lit: born during the second half of the night. Syn: Hiraab, Hiraabe
Hiyood *name-unisex* sense, heart, center of emotion; longing, yearning, hankering; to be aroused or become emotional
Hodan[92] *name-f* wealthy, rich; get wealthy, become rich
Hodman *name-f* wealthy, rich; get wealthy, become rich
Hogol *name-unisex* rain cloud; rainfall
Horaad *name-f* first born daughter; clever, articulate, bright
Hoobaan *name-unisex* ripe fruit
Hoodo *name-f* luck, good fortune. Syn: Ayaan, Cawo, Naruuro
Hoolif *nickname-m* wooly hair, thick ruffled hair. Lit: he who has such hair
Hoombaro *name-f* dolphin
Horor *nickname-m* wild, selfish; greedy

---

[91] **Hibo** Maxamed Huddoon (well-known legendary Somali singer)
[92] **Hodan** Cabdi Walanwal (a legendrry romantic female figure)

Huburow[93] *nickname-m* sweet. Lit: very sweet fruits
Hufan *name-f* winnowed; clean, clear, decent
Hunri *nickname-m* steam, hot vapor: always hot and temperamental person. Cf: Oomaar
Hurfe *nickname-m* darker and stronger
Hurre *nickname-m* black; darker
Huruuse *name-m* black; darker
Huryo *nickname; name-f* small bird sp; humming bird

I

Ibrow *name-m* Ibraahim or Abraham; father of many nations
Idardoon *nickname; name-m* beneficiary
Idigfacle *nickname-m* happier; very social, upbeat
Idil *name-f* all, complete, whole, entire. cf: Dhammo
Idilo *name-f* all, complete, whole, entire
Idman *name-f* permitted, authorized; lit: authorized by God
Iftiimo *name-f* daylight; daytime. Lit: born in daytime
Iftiin *name-unisex* light; enlightenment
Igman *name-f* elected
Iidaan *name-m* dressing, seasoned, spiced
Iidle *name-m* holiday, feast, blessed, festival; lit: the one born during a religious holiday. Syn: Iido, Iidow
Iido *name-f* holiday, feast, blessed, festival. Lit: the one born during a religious holiday. Syn: Iidle, Iidow
Iidow *name-m* holiday, feast, blessed, festival. Lit: the one born during a religious holiday. Syn: Iidle, Iido
Iimaan *name-unisex* belief, faith; confidence, contentment (Arb)
Ijaabo *name-f* acceptance, consent 'in a religious sense' (Arb)
Ilbuur *nickname-m* the one with the protruding eye
Ileeye *name-m* one-eyed, evil-eyed; curser. Syn: Ilkudeeble
Ilkudeeble *nickname-m* evil-eyed; curser. Syn: Ileeye
Ilroon *name-f* better than
Ilwaad *name-f* beauty, attractiveness, prettiness

---

[93] **Huburow** (a singer who sings both Maxay & Maay dialects of the Somali language)

Ilyabar *name-m* eye-gifter
Indhadeeq *nickname; name-f* pleasing to the eyes
Indhayare *nickname-m* small-eyed
Indhawroon *name-f* satisfying to the eyes
Irib *name-m* very small; premature. Cf: Dhicis
Isaaq[94] *name-m* he who pervaded; lit: the one whose mother lost her sensations or became uncounscious upon his delivery. Cf: Saaqa
Isburaash *nickname-m* very clean and very handsome
Ishaar *name-m* point out, indicate, signify (Arb)
Ishaaro *name-f* indication, sign, omen (Arb)
Isir *name-f* ancestry, genealogy, forebears; genetics
Ilkaag *name-f* beautiful, pretty
Islaan *name-m* old man; chief, headman
Islaam *name-m* Islam
Islaaw *name-m* chieftain. Syn: Islow
Islow *name-m* chieftain. Syn: Islaaw
Ismahaan *name-f* most exalted, ruler (Arb)
Ismoog *nickname; name-f* absent minded
Isniino *name-f* Monday; lit: he who was born on a Monday
Istaahil *name-f* value, worth; deserve, be worthy
Istar *name-f* be of use to each other or oneself
Isxal *name-m* self-cleaner; he who solves his own problems; wise man; self-improver

J

Jaajumow *nickname-m* constraint, coercion; forcer, coercer, constrainer
Jaamac[95] *name-m* the Koran (the Islamic religious book as a publication); place of worship, principal mosque of a town. Cf: Masxaf
Jaan-go'an *nickname-m* planned, projected, designed
Jaawe *name-m* aromatic incense, benzion, camphor. Lit: the

---

[94] One of the main Somali clan-confederacies
[95] Sahra Axmed **Jaamac** (well-known female singer)

aromatic one
Jacjuun *nickname-m* cold – an unfriendly person
Jadeer *name-m* plant sp., used for grazing; long journey. Lit: born at an environment filled with such a plant sp., or born during a long trek
Jagfe *nickname-m* a short person. Cf: Cirfe
Jalaf *nickname-m* marauder
Jalaqsan *name-f* soft, sultry beauty, shiny
Jamaad *name-f* sweetness, cuteness, charm
Jambeel *name-m* shield, defense
Jawaahir *name-f* gem, jewel; precious. Syn: Jawharad, Jawhar, Joharad, Jowhar, Joohaar
Jawhar *name-m* gem, jewel; precious. Syn: Jawaahir, Jawharad, Joharad, Jowhar, Joohaar
Jawharad *name-f* gem, jewel; precious. Syn: Jawaahir, Jawhar, Joharad, Jowhar, Joohaar
Jeebo *nickname-m* precise incision; cur, torn, break
Jeebbo *nickname-m* hand-cuffed (Italian)
Jeegaan *name-unisex* arc, arch; rainbow; spectrum
Jeenicad *nickname-m* one who has a white scar/mark on the knee
Jees *name-m* isolated; isolated settlement, hamlet. Lit: born in an isolated settlement
Jeylaani *name-m* land with hard soil. Lit: he who was born in a land with hard soil. Cf: Dhooddi, Jilaani
Jeyte *nickname-m* stronger
Jibraan *name-m* raised; elevated
Jidgooye *nickname-m* bandit (highway robber)
Jiijo *name-f* Khadija; corrupted form of the Arabic name of Khadija
Jiilaal *name-m* winter; cool dry season (born during that season)
Jiir *nickname; name-m* overrun; lean; mouse
Jiiraan *name-m* neighor; lit: he who was born at the home of a neighbor
Jilicow *nickname; name-m* soft, flexible, tender, supple; easy; sick, weak
Jimcaale *name-m* Friday; lit: the one born born on a Friday. Cf: Jimco
Jimco *name-f* Friday; lit: the one born on Friday. Cf: Jimcaale

Jinaw *name-f* sour camel's milk; prospered. Syn: Jinnow
Jiniqow *nickname-m* flexible
Jinnoole *nickname-m* mad, insane; a person possessed by an evil spirit
Jinnow *name-f* sour camel's milk; prospered. syn: Jinaw
Jirde *nickname-m* strong man
Jirroon *name-f* generous, kindly and happy
Johorad *name-f* gem, jewel; precious. Syn: Jawaahir, Jawhar, Jawharad, Jowhar
Jowhar *name-m* gem, jewel; precious. Syn: Jawaahir, Jawhar, Jawharad, Johorad
Joocaar *nickname-m* a very temperamental person
Joof[96] *nickname-m* thick, upright-standing hair. Lit: a man with a thick upright-standing hair
Joogdheer *name-f* tall and straight; beautiful
Joohaar *name-m* legendary serpent-- mythical snake (said to have a jewels in its body that shine at night); Pl: the illuminated stones it leaves behind
Jooqle *nickname-m* elegance, finery, splendor. Cf: Mardaadi, Maruudi, Xarrago
Jug[97] *name-m* bump, bang (sound of hitting). Lit: named after the splash sound of his birth. Cf: Bashka

K

Kaaba *name-f* mend, patch; support
Kaabe *name-m* mend, patch; support
Kaad *name-unisex* doorpost, jamp; warm night; calm hot night. Lit: born at the doorpost or born in a calm hot night.
Kaaha *name-f* ray, first glimmer of light; begin to glow ~ shine. Lit: she who shines the world with happiness
Kaafi *name-m* sufficiency; sufficient. Syn: Kaafiya (Arb)
Kaafiya *name-f* sufficiency; sufficient. Syn: Kaafi (Arb)
Kaahin *name-m* fortune-teller, diviner, soothsayer (Arb)

---
[96] Maxamed Jaamac **Joof** (legendary singer)
[97] See **Bashka**

Kaahiye *name-m* he who shines or enlightens
Kaamil *name-m* whole, complete, entire; entirety (Arb)
Kaariye[98] *nickname; name-m* fare-collector, loading assistant.
   Lit: born while his father was a fare-collector by career or
   he who his labor-pains throbs his mothers's belly badly.
   Cf: Kaarshe, Muunye, Muuddey
Kaarshe *name-m* sudden, sharp pain, throbbing; he who was born
   after a long period of painful and difficult labor. Cf:
   Muuddey or Muunye
Kabaharag *nickname-m* he whom his shoes were made from
   hides or animal skin; hided-shoes
Kablalax *name-m* prosperer, good omen, goodness, welfared,
   good fortune, blessed
Kadab *name-m* share, lot; divine providence, destiny
Kadin[99] *name-m* door, entrance; enclosure for livestock
Kadiye *name-m* surprise, unexpected. Lit: one born unexpectedly
Kalamagood *nickname-m* separated by blood-feud; divided. Lit:
   dispersed or disunited
Karaama *name-m* blessing, divine favor, charisma, supernatural
   power; miracle Arb)
Karaamo *name-f* blessing, divine favor, charisma, supernatural
   power; miracle (Arb)
Karahaye *nickname-m* boiler, steamer; lit: very a temperamental or
   hot-tempered person
Karanle *name-m* rain falling at the end of the cool season, before
   the main autumn rains; feast, banquet; unbroken camel
Karar *nickname-m* downpour, cloudburst, heavy rain
Karuur *name-m* sour camel's milk; prospered
Karruuro *name-f* sour camel's milk; prospered
Kaskiqabe *nickname; name-m* self-conscious; confident
Kasheenle *name-m* specked, speckled, spotted, marked, stained.
   Lit: he who was born with birth-marks. Syn: Barre, Barrey,
   Barrow
Kawtama *nickname-f* pepple-toss game player; juggler

---

[98] Maxamed Cali **Kaariye** (well-known playwright & poet)
[99] Jaamac Biixi **Kadin** (surviving Dervish who witnessed British war
planes attacking the Dervish citadel of Taleex toward the end of 1920)

Kawtame *nickname-m* pepple-toss game player; juggler
Kawte *nickname-m* pepple-toss game player; juggler
Kayd *name-m* reserve, preserved, set a side, deposit; substitute
Kaynaan *name-m* emigration, continuous travel towards a specific destination; caravan. Lit: one born during that kind of travel
Kaytoon *nickname-m* tall and thin
Kediye[100] *name-m* surprise, unexpected. Lit: one born unexpectedly and suddenly
Keenadiid[101] *nickname; name-m* slavery refuter. Lit: he who refuses to be led to unwanted direction
Keyse *name-m* prosperity
Khadan *name-f* good luck; lucky charm, amulet (Arb). Syn: Qadan
Khadar *name-m* holy man, saint; fortune, luck. Cf: Khadaro, Khadro
Khadaro *name-f* holy woman, saint; fortune, luck (Arb). Syn: Khadar, Khadro
Khadro *name-f* holy man, saint; fortune, luck. Cf: Khadar, Khadaro
Khaladla' *name-f* errorless; straight; righteous. Syn: Qaladla'
Khalaf *name-m* caliph; Khaliif (Arb)
Khayr *name-m* goodness, good fortune, welfare, blessing
Khayrre *name-m* good fortune, welfare, blessing. Syn: Khayro
Khayro *name-f* goodness, good fortune, welfare, blessing. Syn: Khayrre
Kifaayo *name-f* sufficiency; satisfaction; enough (Arb)
Kifaax *name-m* struggle
Kiin *name-f* beautiful; friendly; sociable
Kinsi[102] *name-f* high caste; prosperity, well-being
Koraad *name-f* waiting, expecting
Kor-dahab *name-unisex* gold skinned; skin of gold
Koron *nickname; name-m* gelded
Koobe *name-m* summarizer, coiler (mispronounced as Koombe)
Koomade *name-m* visionary; very far-sighted

---

[100] Jaamac **Kediye** Cilmi (highly acclaimed poet)
[101] Suldaan Yuusuf Cali **Keenadiid** (Sultan of Hobyo)
[102] **Kinsi** Xaaji Aadan (well-known singer)

Koore *nickname-m* sadldle; saddler
Kooreeye *nickname-m* saddler
Koos *name-f* continent; earth. Cf: Aasiya
Koosaar *name-unisex* seasoning, condiment, gravy, relish
Kooshin *name-m* praiseworthy; spoiled
Kul *name-m* heat
Kulan *name-m* unification, meeting, assembly, encounter; large evergreen tree sp. lit: born while his immediate family is in meeting or born under a Kulan tree. Syn: Kullane
Kullane *name-m* meeting, assembly, encounter; large evergreen tree sp., Lit: one born while his immediate family is in meeting or born under a Kulan tree. Syn: Kulan
Kulmis *name-unisex* convening; convener
Kulmiye *name-m* one who holds a meeting, convener. Lit: having Many relatives or followers convened at his birth or one conceived unexpectedly
Kuluc[103] *nickname-m* a fatty person; plump
Kunciil *name-m* thousands-disturber. Lit: he who at his birth makes too many people of his kinsmen anxious; or who at his birth causes a bitter resentment to his enemy
Kutubey *nickname; name-f* religious
Kuukaay *nickname-m* person with a flat-nose and kink hair; i.e. a Negro
Kuusow *nickname; name-m* rounded, globular, lumpy; stocky, short

L

Laacdo *name-f* greenery; burgeon
Lacago *name-f* silvery; rich
Ladan *name-f* healthy, good, fine, well; wealthy
Ladane *name-m* healthy, good, fine, well; wealthy
Lafaqaab *nickname; name-m* bone healer. Lit: traditional orthopedist
Lajecel *name-f* loved one
Laymuun *name-f* sweet—said of females

---

[103] Maxamed Axmed **Kuluc** (well-known legend singer)

Lebi *nickname; name-unisex* tall and handsome or beautiful like the tall tree specie of *lebi* and its beautiful flowers
Leelkase *nickname-m* farsighted, mindful, smart, very intelligent
Leexo *name-f* swing; hammock; tornado, cyclone, whirlwind
Libaax *name-m* lion; brave; hero
Libin *name-unisex* victory; victor; victorious. Cf: Guuleed
Limaan *name-m* loving
Lisaan *name-m* tongue (Arb)
Lisan *name-f* milked; extracted ~ squeezed out
Liibaan *name-m* success, victory, glory, triumph; to come to a successful end, win, be victorious, succeed
Liibaangashe *nickname; name-m* victorious; victory bearer
Lo'doon *name-m* cattle seeker
Looboge *nickname; name-m* beloved one
Looga *name-f* hosting; slaughterer
Looge *name-m* hosting; slaughterer
Looyaan *nickname; name-m* unrest, agitation, turbulence. Lit: named after the baby who was restless and too hyper while he was in his mother's womb or he who remains too hyper and restless after birth
Loxos *name-m* new settlement, place ~ house; spend the night for the first time in a new area
Lubbi *name-f* heart, core; desire, good feelings; intelligence (Arb)
Luwaay *name-m* powerful; strong
Luul[104] *name-f* precious, pearl, diamond; gems grinder
Luula *name-f* precious, pearl, diamond; gems grinder

M

Maad *name-m* joker; funny remarks; comic or comedy
Maadey *name-m* Muhammad
Maahir name-f adventurer, explorer
Maalin *name-m* day; daylight; proven; clear; very visible
Maana *name-f* mindful; intelligence; good sense

---

[104] **Luul** Jeylaani (singer)

Maana-faay *name-f* mindfulness; mentally fit and healthy; intellectual (the mindful Fatima; or Fatima, the mindful)
Maandeeq[105] *name-m/f* handsome, beautiful; gratifying
Maasheeye *name-m* drowner; overwhelmer
Maaweel[106] *nickname-m* entertainer; amuser
Maax *name-m* flow, gush (of water); to be full (said of a well); produce, create
Mabeeneeye *nickname-m* truthful, trustworth
Macaane *name-m* sweetie (as a term of endearment)
Macallin *name-m* teacher; educator; instructor
Macalow name-m dew lapper; double chinned
Macow *name-m* to become sweet; to become tender in nature; mellow
Madar *name-m* kindness, mercy, mercifulness; meeting place, gathering. Lit: he who was born while his kinsmen are gathering or was born at the gathering place
Madarkicis *name-m* gathering agitator, meeting disrupter
Madaxey *name-m* chief, boss, official; or he whose head was disproportional to his body frame at birth
Madhibaan *nickname-m* harmless, very decent one
Madhiin *name-f* deep red color; lit: beautiful with bright light-skin. Syn: Dhiimo, Dhiin
Madiino *name-f* Medina; lit: one named after the Islamic holy city of Medina. Cf: Mino
Madoobe *nickname; name-m* black, swarthy
Magadle *nickname; name-m* tanned hide, leather; tanning substance
Magan[107] *name-m* refuge. Lit: he who is a refugee to Allah
Magool[108] *name-f* germination, sprouting, bud, new growth or prosperity
Maha *name-m* cool and quiet (Danakil)
Mahad *name-m* thanks; gratitude

---

[105] Faadumo Cabdullaahi **Maandeeq** (legendary singer)
[106] Maxamed Aadan **Maaweel** (poet)
[107] Xirsi **Magan** Ciise (Somali literary scholar & story-teller)
[108] Xaliimo Khaliif **Magool** (most popular & golden-voiced Somali female singer)

Mahad-Alle *name-m* thanks to Allah; gratitude to God
Mahadle *name-m* gratitude
Mahado *name-f* thanks; gratitude
Majabe *name-m* unbreakable; brave; strong
Majeerteen[109] *name-f* attraction; longing; to be strongly attracted to; longing for in one's heart
Makahaan *name-m* very patient; low-tempered
Makaraan *name-unisex* amulet
Mako *name-f* Mecca. Lit: named after the Islamic holy city of Mecca
Malabo *name-f* honey; sweet
Mamaasan *name-m* prosperer
Maqaarre *name-m* skin, pelt, hide, scalp
Mardaaddi *name-m; nickname* elegance; to be elegant. Cf: Maruudi, Xarrago
Markabo *name-f* ship. Lit: one born over-weight
Marraaxaan *name-m* sling, catapult; restless; hurler, thrower. Cf: Marreexaan, Marriixaan, Warfaa
Marreexaan *name-m* sling, catapult; restless; hurler, thrower. Cf: Marraaxaan, Marriixaan, Warfaa
Marriixaan name-m *m* sling, catapult; restless; hurler; thrower. Cf: Marraaxaan, Marreexaan, Warfaa
Martile *name-m* guest-keeper
Maruudi *name-m; nickname* elegance; to be elegant. Cf: Mardaadi
Marwo *name-f* lady, an honorable woman; Mrs.; respectful term for women. Syn: Murwo
Maryaad *name-f to* be agitated; to become restless; to get confused or she who was born with mental confusion; restlessness due to emotion or unbearable labor pains for her mother. Cf: Meryaad or Miryaad
Maslax[110] *name-m* peace-maker, conciliator. Syn: Samakaab, Samawada, Samawade

---

[109] Xaaji Cali **Majeerteen** (mystic & reformer who was a scholar in both Islamic scriptures & Somali literature; lived approximately between 1770-1838)
[110] Cali Xasan Cali **Maslax** (one of the surviving thirteen founders of the Somali Youth League)

Masxaf[111] *name-m* the Koran; the Islamic religious book as a publication. Cf: Jaamac (Arb)
Mataan *name-m* twin
Maxamed-deeq *name-m* honorable and generous
Mayal *name-m* the handle of the sheild
Maye *name-m* refuter; rejecter; opposed; he who apposes
Mayle *name-m* refuter; rejecter; opposed; he who apposes
Mayra *name-f* she who cleanses; purifies; blessed one
Mayran *name-f* washed; cleansed
Mayrane *name-m* washed; cleansed
Meecaaddo *name-f* advantage; lasting value; reserved for the future; prosperity; fortune; name of a star (considered a sign of good fortune). Cf: Fartuun
Meecaad[112] *name-m* advantage; lasting value; reserved for the future; prosperity; fortune; name of a star (considered a sign of good fortune). Cf: Fartuun
Meryaad *name-f* to be agitated; to become restless; to be confused or she who was born with mental confusion; restlessness due to strong emotion or unbearable birth-pains for her mother during delivery. Cf: Maryaad or Miryaad
Meygaag *name-m* evergreen; he who was born under the evergreen Meygaag tree
Midgaan *nickname-m* skillful; hunter; sharpshooter
Migil *name-m* germination, sprouting, bud, new growth or prosperity
Miido *name-f* sweet juice
Miiggan *name-f* sturdy, durable; honest, direct, reliable. Syn: Miiggane
Miiggane *name-m* sturdy, durable; honest, direct, reliable. Syn: Miiggan
Mikadoor *name-m* very active and clever; the best
Milgo *name-f* germination, sprouting, bud, new growth or prosperity
Mina *name-f* fortunate (Arb)

---

[111] Daa'uud Cali **Masxaf** (guitarist and lyricist who sings occasionally)
[112] **Meecaad** Miiggane Aw-Maacaleesh (well-known comedian & songwriter)

Mire *name-m* occurer; comer of the middle of the night. Lit: he who was born in the middle of the night
Mirifle *nickname-m* dust-particler
Miiran *name-f* Serene; healthy; sound of mind, sane, mentally lucid
Miryaad *name-f* be agitated; become restless; get confused, or she who was born with mental confusion, restlesness due to emotion or the unbearable pain her mother experienced during child-birth. Cf: Maryaad, Meryaad
Misbaax *name-f* lantern, lamp Arb)
Misirre *nickname-m* he who collects large pieces of fire woods by profession
Miski *name-f* musk; aromatic (Arb)
Miyir *name-unisex* awareness, consciousness, intelligence, intellect; care
Miyirwalaal *name-m* aware; articulate; cool-tempered
Mohorre *name-m* half; incomplete
Mohoro *name-f* half; incomplete
Mooge[113] *nickname; name-m* ignorant, unaware; absent-minded, lacking
Moolkaal *name-m* save-guard
Mooracase *nickname-m* coral-red; he whose corral (pen) was built with large reddish stones
Moorasaante *nickname-m* coral sentry, guide; pen guide
Moorgan[114] *nickname-m* sharpshooter; sometimes confused with the english name of Morgan
Muddulood *nickname-m* unified; united
Mudub *name-m* black; darck; soft
Mulki *name-f* ownership; personal property (Arb)
Mullaaxo *name-f* bark fiber used for making string or rope. lit: Smooth and beautiful
Muraayad *name-f* mirror; glass. Syn: Mandarad Cf: Biladdaya
Muraayo *name-f* mirror; glass. syn: Mandarad. Cf: Biladdaya

---

[113] Maxamed **Mooge** Liibaan & Axmed **Mooge** Liibaan (two well-known singer brothers)
[114] Gen. Maxamed Siciid Xirsi **Moorgan** (Somali general who is best known for his sharp-shooting skills)

Murriyad *name-f* gold-beaded necklace; sultry beauty
Murriyo *name-f* gold-beaded necklace; sultry beauty
Muruqle nickname-m muscle-bound; a strongly-built man
Murursade *nickname-m* angry, resentful, sulking; repentance, regret
Murwo *name-f* lady, honorable woman; Mrs.; respectful term for women. Syn: Marwo
Muxumud[115] *name-m* honorable, praised, praise-worthy; corrupted form of Arabic name of Muxamad or Maxamuud
Muuddey *name-m* one who moves slowly and with difficulty; he who was born after a long period of painful and difficult labor. Cf: Kaarshe or Muunye
Muumin *name-m* a real and true Muslim believer
Muumino *name-f* a real and true Muslim
Muunye *name-m* sudden, sharp pain, throbbing; he who was born after a long period of painful and too difficult labor. Cf: Muuddey, Kaarshe)

N

Naado *name-f* slogan; announcement; war-cry
Naalleeye *name-m* bringer of good fortune, news or happy tidings; an unforgettable moment or occasion
Naalleeyo *name-f* bringer of good fortune, news or happy tidings; an unforgettable moment or occasion
Nabaad *name-f* vegetation, plantlife
Nabdoon *name-f* well, peaceful, secure
Nadiif *name-m* clean, pure. Syn: Nadiifo
Nadiifo *name-f* clean, pure. Syn: Nadiif
Nagaad *name-f* permanence, stability; make stable or permanent. Cf: Negeeye. Syn: Negaad
Naqiib *nickname; name-m* arbitrator, deal with a legal case
Naruuro *name-f* luck, fate, good fortune. Syn: Ayaan, Cawo,

---

[115] Cabdi **Muxumud** Ammiin (well-known playwright, poet & legendary singer; best known by his Land Cruiser play against Barre's dictatorship in late 1980s.)

Nasiib
Nasiib *name-Unisex* luck, fate, good fortune. Syn: Ayaan, Cawo, Naruuro
Nasra *name-f* Victoria; success, victory, good fortune (Arb)
Nasri *name-unisex* success, victory, good fortune (Arb)
Nasteexo *name-f* advice, counsel, comfort
Naxariiswaaq *name-m* sky God's mercy
Nediboore *name-m* whip-craft; whipper
Negeeya *name-f* to make stable; calm down, cause to become calm and serene. Cf: Negaad, Negeeye
Negeeye[116] *name-m to* make stable; calm down, to cause to become calm serene. Cf: Negaad, Negeeya
Negaad *name-f* permanence, stability; make stable or permanent. Cf: Negeeye. Syn: Nagaad
Negi *name-f* stable, firm; permamently settled; calm, serene
Neyruus *name-f* bonfire, feast on the occasion of the Somali and/or Persian Solar New Year (usually in early August). Lit: she who was born during this celebratory occasion
Nimcaad *name-m* natural resource; prosperity, abundance
Nimcaale *name-m* natural resource; prosperity, abundance
Nimco[117] *name-f* natural resource; prosperity, abundance (Arb)
Noolays *name-m* reviving, keeping alive, resurrecting, nourisher
Nooleeya *name-f* reviving, keeping alive, resurrecting, nourisher
Nuur[118] *name-m* light; to give light, shine. Syn: Nuuro, Nuurre, Nuurto
Nuureey *name-m* shiner; to give off light, to shine. Syn: Nuur, Nuuro, Nuurto
Nuuriya *name-f* to light up, to cause to shine
Nuuriye *name-m* to light up, to cause to shine
Nuuro *name-f* light; to give off light, to shine. Syn: Nuur, Nuurre, Nuurto
Nuurre *name-m* shiner; to give off light, to shine. Syn: Nuur, Nuuro, Nuurto
Nuurto *name-f* shiner; to give off light, to shine. Syn: Nuur, Nuuro,

---

[116] Cabdulqaadir Xasan **Negeeye** (singer & playwright)
[117] **Nimco** Jaamac (sweet-voiced Djiboutian leading female singer)
[118] **Nuur** Cilmi 'Daalacay' (young Djiboutian singer)

O

Odawaa *name-m* an orphan; he who misses his father. Lit: one born after his father died while he was still in his mother's womb

Ogaad *nickname-unisex* discoverer; to find out; get to know; become aware or realize; look after; take care of; knowledgeable; aware. Lit: he/she who takes care of or looks after another

Ogaadeen *nickname-m* discoverer; to find out; get to know; become aware or realize; look after; take care of. Lit: he who takes care of or looks after another

Olol[119] *name-m* flame, fire; to cry out (said of a he-camel in heat); handsome, very light-kinned

Oogle *nickname; name-m* to kindle, to light a fire; to drive, to urge on; high flames; early dawn. Lit: troublesome or he who was born early in the morning or at dawn

Oomaar *nickname; name-m* steam, emit steam; mist, vapor. Lit: an always hot and temperamental person or he who was born during the hot and windy season. Cf: Hunri

Oomman *name-f* thirsty; drought, waterless season, waterless place; she who was born during a drought spell or was born in a drought-striken place

Oommane *name-m* thirsty, drought, waterless season; waterless place; he who was born during a drought spell or was born in a drought-striken place

Oontira *name-f* thirst reliever

Oontire *name-m* thirst reliever

Orshe *nickname-m* noise-maker, clamor; rhythmic chanter

Q

---

[119] **Olol** Diinle (Biyamaal chieftain of Lower Jubba during the colonial era)

Qaabbil *nickname; name-unisex* welcome, receive; face, encounter, confront; front; approach
Qaafo *name-unisex* leader, chief; respectable, important
Qaaje *nickname-m* pale white (color of a horse); pale-whitish person; which is considered by some as beautiful
Qaali *name-f* dear, costly
Qaanso *name-f* bow; arch; bracket
Qaareey *nickname-m* cudgel, club, bat. Lit: he who is accustomed as carrying a club
Qaayaweyn *name-f* important, significant, valuable
Qaayib *name-m* he who follows new fashions; adaptable
Qaayiba *name-f* she who follows new fashions; stylish
Qadan *name-f* good luck; lucky charm, amulet (Arb). Syn: Khadan
Qadiid *nickname; name-m* kinky haired; wood used for smoking milk vessel or the black color it produces (black)
Qadow *name-f* edible fruits of parasitic plant sp., stands for beauty
Qalaad *nickname-m* foreign, exotic, strange. Lit: someone who has strange manners
Qaladla' *name-f* corrected, errorless; straight; righteous. Syn: Qaladla', Saxan
Qalanjo[120] *nickname; name-f* female ~ cow elephant; actress. Lit: beautiful and well-behaved
Qalbi *name-f* heart, core; desire, good feelings; intelligence (Arb)
Qalinle[121] *nickname-m* silvery. Lit: a man whose tooth or teeth are coated with silvery material
Qamaan *name-m* crowd, throng; extreme need or desire
Qamar *name-f* moon (Arb)
Qarad *name-f* scope, objective, purpose
Qardabo *nickname-m* trouble, distress. Lit: troublemaker
Qase *nickname-m* disturber; troublesome
Qawdhan *nickname; name-m* noisemaker
Qayaad *nickname-m* brave, clever
Qaybe *name-m* memorizer. Lit: he who learns by heart
Qaylo *nickname-m* shouter, yeller; clamor, noise
Qaylow *nickname; name-m* yell, yeller, shouter; clamor, noise. Lit:

---

[120] Khadiijo **Qalanjo** (folklore dancer who sings occasionally)
[121] Muuse Ismaaciil **Qalinle** (singer)

one named after his yelling noise at birth
Qoomaal[122] *nickname; name-m* annoyer, disturber
Qoordheer *nickname; name-unisex* long-necked (very beautiful or handsome)
Qoorsheel *nickname-m* double-chinned (considered a mark of beauty)
Qoran *name-f* carved; sharpened, pointed; proportionate
Qorrax *name-m* sun; daylight; sun-rays. Syn: Cadceed, Gabbal
Qorraxo *name-f* sun; daylight; sun-rays
Qubeys *name-m* bathed, bath, showering
Qulubeen *name-m* disturbed, gloomy, depressed
Qumman *name-f* righteous. Syn: Qummane
Qummane *name-m* righteous. Syn: Qumman
Qurac *name-m* acacia tree. Lit: born under an acacia tree.
Qureysho *name-f* high caste; a highl-born woman. Lit: named after Prophet Muhammad's Qureysh clan. Cf: Gobey, Gobaad
Quulle *name-m* wild nut; lit: born closeby or an environment full of that wild nut-tree

R

Rabbiile *name-m* one who belongs to or is beloved by Allah. Cf: Allaale
Raage[123] *name-m* Saturn (the sixth planet): the durable, longe-lived. Lit: the long-staying one
Raagsan *name-f to* be durable; live long. Lit: the long-staying one (may you live long!)
Raalliyo *name-f* kind woman; agreeable ~ loyal wife
Raaxo *name-f* pleasure, comfort, convenience
Racwi *name-f* fatty and heavy at birth
Rafle *nickname-m* the restless one because of physical discomfort
Rako *name-f* platform, shelf, scaffolding
Ramad *name-f* newly delivered female camel. Lit: lovely

---

[122] Maxamed Axmed **Qoomaal** (musician, lyricist and singer who sings both **Maxay** & **Maay** dialects of the Somali language)
[123] **Raage** Ugaas (legendary sultan and poet)

Rasaas *name-m* ammunition, bullet, cartridge; brass. Cf: Xabad (Arb)
Raxmo *name-f* kindness, mercy, mercifulness
Raydab *name-m* tall tree (taller)
Raydabo *name-f* tall tree (taller)
Reegow *name-m* long-lasting; live-long
Riiraash *nickname-m* unreserveable; unpreserveable; undepositable
Riyaale *name-m* goat owner; rail, thaler
Riyaaq *name-f* joy, happiness, enthusiasm. Cf: Farax, Faarax, Farxaan
Rooble *name-m* rain-maker; he who was born at a rainy seaon
Roobo *name-f* rain-maker; she who was born at the rainy season
Roon *name-f* better (off ~ than); good, excellent, superior
Roone *name-m* better (off ~ than); good, excellent, superior
Rooraaye *nickname-m* stampede; runner
Rooxaan *name-f* evil spirits believed to possess people and cause sickness
Rooxo *name-f* climbing plant sp., with edible fruit. Lit: sweet
Rummaan *name-f* colorful; pomegranate
Ruun *name-f* home, settlement, dwelling-place. Lit: one born at Home

S

Saafi[124] *name-f* cleanliness; purity, pure, clean
Saado[125] *name-f* prediction, prophecy, good omen; provisions, supplies
Saahid[126] *name-m* ascetic person (Arb)
Saaqa *name-f* she who pervaded. Lit: the one whose mother lost her sensations after this child is delivered; she who goes unconscious at birthing. Cf: Isaaq
Saaxiib *name-m* friend, companion

---

[124] **Saafi** Ducaale (singer)
[125] **Saado** Cali Warsame (well-known singer)
[126] **Saahid** Qamaan (legendary poet)

Sabriye[127] *name-m* to counsel patience; to help some one to be patient
Sabti *name-m* Saturday. Lit: one born on a Saturday
Sabtiye *name-m* Saturday. Lit: one born on a Saturday
Sacad *nickname; name-m* white cow
Sacmaal *name-m* he who milks cows; cow milker
Sade *name-m* generious, giver of food; host; distributor. Syn: Sooraan, Soore
Sagal *name-f* rays of light at dawn (which indicates a distant rain). Lit: one born with beauty; sunshine
Sahal *name-m* ease, easiness, simplicity; easy, simple, uncomplicated
Sahlan *name-f* ease, easiness, simplicity; easy, simple, uncomplicated
Salaad[128] *name-m* prayer. Lit: blessed. Syn: Salaado
Salaado *name-f* prayer. Lit: blessed. Syn: Salaad
Salaan[129] *name-m* greeting; salutation
Salaw *nickname-m* shouting, uproar. Syn: Salow, Salwe, Sooyaan
Salow *nickname-m* shouting, uproar. Syn: Salaw, Salwe, Sooyaan
Saluugla' *name-f* irrefutable, undeniable
Salwe *nickname-m* shouting, uproar. Syn: Salaw, Salwe, Sooyaan
Salwo *name-f* shouting, uproar. Lit: one named after her loud cry at birth
Samaale *name-m* peaceable, kind, fortunate; high caste. Cf: Gobaad, Gobey
Samakaab *name-m* peace maker, conciliator. Lit: supporter of the right way. Syn: Maslax, Samawade, Samawada
Samaroon *name-m* kindness, goodness, favor
Samatalis *name-m* good counselor
Samatar[130] *name-m* doer of good, humanitarian, philanthropist
Samawada *name-f* peace maker, conciliator. Syn: Maslax, Samakaab, Samawade

---

[127] **Sabriye** (musician who plays the piano)
[128] **Salaad** Maxmed Shardi 'Darbi' (well-known singer)
[129] **Salaan** Carrabey (legendary poet)
[130] Xasan Aadan **Samatar** (well-known singer)

Samawade *name-m* peace maker, conciliator. Syn: Maslax, Samakaab, Samawada
Same *name-m* kindness, goodness; favors
Saransoor *name-m* joining, joint, point where two things meet
Sardheeye *nickname-m* nap-taker, sleep-head. Lit: he who is accustomed to taking a nap or short snooze frequently
Sareedo *name-f* good fortune; prosperity. Lit: she who was born at a time of plenty. Syn: Barwaaqo, Doonbiro
Sariir *name-m* bed; very patient one
Saruur *name-m* happy (Arb)
Saxan *name-f* correct. Syn: Qaladla
Saxansaxo *nickname; name-unisex* cool breeze just prior to a rainstorm. Lit: simple person by nickname or he who his parents/relatives were overjoyed by his birth
Saxardiid *name-m* cleanness; pure
Saxarla' *name-f* the one without fault). Syn: Ceebla'
Saylaan *nickname-m* vibration; front of a passing rain, quick passing rain. Syn: Dhool
Sayid[131] *nickname; name-m* lord; excellence (Arb). Syn: Shariif
Saylici[132] *name-m* Somali traditional dance. Lit: he who was born while that kind of dance was performed
Sayruuq *nickname-m* rocket, missile. Lit: fast runner
Seed *nickname-m* tendon, nerve; strong; rigid
Seefle *nickname-m* sword-bearer; warrior; fighter
Seeraar *nickname-m* he who throws something out of sight (i.e., over a wall). Lit: someone who marauds around unexpectedly; restless person. Cf: Warfaa
Shaaciya *nickname; name-f* spread, diffuse, propagate; divulge; cause to glare; reveal, bring to light
Shaaciye *nickname; name-m* spread, diffuse, propagate; divulge; cause to glare; reveal, bring to light
Shabeel *nickname; name-m* leopard; wild cat
Shabeelow *nickname; name-m* leopard; wild cat

---

[131] **Sayid** Maxamed Cabdulle Xasan (founder and the leader of the Somali dervish movement 1856-1920)
[132] Sheekh Cabdulraxmaan Axmed **Saylici** (Sufi Tarriqa leader in Northern Somalia who lived between 1820-1882)

Shacni *name-f* beautiful, adorable
Shadoor *name-m* comic; joker
Shahmaad *name-f* amazement, admiration
Shafeec *name-m* favor, good deed. Syn: Shafeeco
Shafeeco *name-f* favor, good deed. Syn: Shafeec
Shammaal *name-m* north wind (Arb)
Shamso *name-f* the sun
Shamuuke *nickname-m* fatty and friendly person
Shankaroon[133] *name-f* better than five
Shaqlan *name-f* decorated, adorned
Sharaf *name-m* handsomeness, grace, splendor, prestige, nobility, honor, pride, reputation, respect
Sharfan *name-f* beauty, grace, splendor, prestige, nobility, honor, pride, reputation, respect
Sharmaarke[134] *name-m* the one who does not see evil
Sheegan *name-f* revealed, claimed, reported
Sheegow *name-m* revealed, claimed, reported
Shibban *nickname; name-f* silent, mum, not talking, quite
Shibbane *nickname; name-m* silent, mum, not talking, quite
Shiidaad[135] *nickname-m* bother, disturbance. Cf: Shiddo
Shiiqow *name-m* shrinked, become deflated~smaller; melt (away)
Shiiraar *name-m* preventor; rejecter; strapper. Syn: Celi
Sheekhdoon *name-m* seeker of Mullahs. Syn: Awdoon
Shiidaad *nickname-m* hard task, tideous work, nuisance, bother
Shiidle *nickname; name-m* grinding stone, millstone, mill; stone
Shiil *nickname-m* heated stone; grill; branding iron. Lit: lacking; temperamental person
Shidan *nickname; name-f* alight (burning)
Shidane *nickname; name-m* alight (burning)
Shiddo *nickname-m* bother, disturbance. Cf: Shiidaad
Shifo *name-f* good health
Shifeeya *name-f* medicinal; she who brings goodness

---

[133] **Shankaroon** Axmed Sagal (singer)
[134] Yaasiin Xaaji Cismaan **Sharmaarke** & Cabdulrashiid Cali **Sharmaarke** (pioneer of the formation of the Somali Youth League; & the first prime minister of the Somali Republic who later became the second president of the republic, respectively)
[135] Cigaal **Shiidaad** (well-known figure in the Somali classical folktales)

Shillin *name-f* large evergreen tree sp., with hard timber and edible fruit. Lit: one born near or under that tree
Shimbir[136] *name-m (nickname)* bird. Cf: Ciyow
Shirdoon *name-m* assembly seeker. Cf: Shirshoore, Shirwac
Shira *name-f* council, assembly
Shire *name-m* council, assembly
Shiriye *name-m* he who brings (people) together. Cf: Gendershe
Shirsoore *name-m* giver of food; host; distributor. Lit: the one who called the meeting. Cf: Shirwac. Syn: Sade, Sooraan, Soore
Shirwac *name-m* convener. Lit: the one who called the meeting. Syn: Shirdoon, Shirshoore
Shoobe *nickname-m* dandy, fop, carefully elegant dresser
Shoobo *nickname-f* dandy, fop, carefully elegant dresser
Shooca *name-f* shinning, lightning, bright
Shooli[137] *nickname-m* boaster, bragger. Syn: Dhoodaan
Shube[138] *nickname-m* poem reciter; orator; talkative
Shukri *name-f* gratitude, thankfullness, thanks (Arb)
Shummey *name-f* kisser, kissing
Shuun *name-f* high caste. Cf: Gobaad, Gobey, Samaale
Shuuriye *nickname-m* haughtiness, obstinate; silent
Sifaad *name-f* one who has a distinguishing mark, characteristic or description
Sifeeya *name-f* cleaner; distinguisher; explainer; he who makes clear or describes clearly. Syn: Sifeeye
Sifeeye *name-m* cleaner; distinguisher; explainer; he who makes clear or describes clearly. Syn: Sifeeya
Sifir *nickname-m* zero, nought. Lit: good for nothing
Siidi *name-m* Saeed or Said; loyal, obedient (Arb)
Siidow *name-m* Saeed or Said; loyal, obedient
Siigaale *nickname-m* dust-maker. Lit: dust colored
Siinwaaq *name-m* sky sky God's gift
Sinji *name-m* origin, descent; race
Siman *name-f* smooth; flat; equal
Siraad *name- unisex* lamp, light; glow, illuminate; light on

---

[136] Maxamed Axmed Good **'Shimbir'** (legendary singer)
[137] Cumar **Shooli** (well-known singer, lyricist & guitarist)
[138] Cabdulqaadir Cabdi **Shube** (playwright, poet & folktaler)

Siwaaqroon *name-m* good thread; good lineage. Cf: Absame
Siyaad *name-m* extra, addition, increase, surplus
Socdaal *name-m* traveler
Sokor *name-m* sugar; sweets. Syn: Sonkor
Sonkor *name-m* sugar; sweets. Syn: Sokor
Soodhacay *name-m* fallen
Soofe[139] *nickname-m* sharpener, whetstone, grindstone
Soohan *name-f* plaited, woven, spun. Lit: proportionate
Soolane *nickname-m* bachelor
Soomman *nickname; name-f* fasting from badness (cleansed)
Soommane *nickname; name-m* fasting from badness (cleansed)
Sooraan[140] *name-m* giver of food; host; distributor. Syn: Sade, Soore
Sooraante *name-m* giver of food; host; distributor. Syn: Sade, Soore
Soore *name-m* giver of food; host; distributor. Syn: Sade, Sooraan
Sooyaan *nickname-m* shouting, uproar. Syn: Salaw, Salwe, Salwo
Subeer *name-m; nickname-m* marauder
Subkan *name-f* anointed, creamed
Sugaal *name-m* waiting, expectation
Sugan *name-f* certain, sure, verified, correct, appropriate, exact, precise; reliable, confirmed
Suge *name-m* certain, sure, verified, correct, appropriate, exact, precise; reliable, confirmed
Sugulle[141] *name-m* black-maned
Suldaan[142] *name-m* sultan, prince
Sulub *name-m* polished; smooth
Sulubo *name-f* polished; smooth
Sunwaaq *name-m* sky God's poison
Sureer *name-f* tall and proportional; sweet, honey
Surad *name-f* medicinal; tall and beauty
Surre *name-m* honey, sweet
Suubban *name-f* good, nice; fair, righteous. Syn: Suubbane

---

[139] Xaliimo **Soofe** (poet)
[140] Cabdullaahi Diiriye **Sooraan** (poet & playwright who also sings occasionally)

[141] Cali **Sugulle** (poet & playwright)
[142] Cabdullaahi **Suldaan** Timacadde (legendary poet)

Suubbane *name-m* good, nice; fair, righteous. Syn: Suubban
Suudi[143] *name-m* heat of the sun. Lit: born during the height of a heat wave
Suufi[144] *name-m* Sufi mystic; adherent to one of the Sufi orders. Lit: one who belongs to Sufism
Suurat *name-f* medicinal; tall and beauty. Syn: Surad
Suuri *name-f* dates originating from Syria. Lit: white. Cf: Barni
Suuryaan *nickname-m* groaner, moaner

T

Taajir[145] *nickname; name-m* rich
Taajiro *nickname; name-f* rich
Taakilo *nickname-m* helper; philanthropic
Tabiile *name-m* skilled, clever, tactful
Tagaalwaaq *name-m* sky God's left-over or gift
Tagallewaaq *name-m* sky God's grace
Tagsan *name-f* gone; past
Tahliil[146] *name-m* blessed; curative; attempter; holy water (which may be blessed by the ink from a Qur'anic text or prayers; it's drunk or sprinkled as a blessing, to cure sickness or protect crops). Lit: he who has been blessed
Takar *nickname-m* gadfly, camel-fly, horse-fly. Lit: temperamental person
Takhal *name-m* post, mast (of a boat)
Takhtar *nickname-m* medical doctor; herbal doctor
Talal *name-m* moan, groan. Syn: Dalal
Talamadar *name-m* good adviser, good counselor
Talamadoor *name-m* obedient, loyal
Talamugge *nickname; name-m* perfect adviser, perfect counselor
Talareer *name-m* leader, counsilor; family's decision, advice, opinion, direction, proposal. Lit: he who was born after his

---

[143] Xaaji **Suudi** (Dervish's foreign envoy)
[144] Sheekh Cali **Suufi** (well-know Sufi mullah)
[145] Axmed Maxamed **Taajir** (BBC London's Somali section correspondent in Nairobi, Kenya)
[146] Cabdi **Tahliil** Warsame (singer, song-writer, lyricist)

father's lineage advised him to marry a particular woman (who born him)

Taliso *name-f* ruler, commander

Taliye *name-m* ruler, commander

Talxe *name-m* easy life (Arb)

Tanaad *name-unisex* to get rich, to be wealthy

Tanade *name-m* to get rich, to be wealthy. Syn: Hodan or Tanaad

Tarrax *name-m* diluter, mixer. lit. he who dilutes

Tawaad *name-m* dark in color or black

Tawllan *name-f* well-formed ~ built, shapely, gorgeous and beautiful

Teesiyow *nickname-m* sharp-shooter

Tiinle *name-m* fig tree; fig ~ figs (fruit). Lit: a man named after that fig tree (Arb)

Tiirshe *nickname; name-m* he who supports his household morally, emotionally and physically

Tigaad *name-f* place with abundant rain ~ green grass; prosperity. Lit: she who was born in such an environment. Cf: Barwaaqo, Doonbiro

Timir *name-m* date-palm tree and/or its fruit; dates. Syn: Timirre, Timiro

Timirre *name-m* date-palm tree or its fruit; dates. Syn: Timir, Timoro

Timiro *name-f* date-palm tree and/or its fruit; dates. Syn: Timir, Timirre

Tiriig *name-f* electric light, torch; lit: sultry beauty

Tisqaad *name-f* to grow-up, increase, multiply; reach adulthood, come of age (said of a youth)

Toddob *name-unisex* beginning of spring, first rain of the wet season

Togane *nickname-m* tall and stretched; tauten

Toljecle *name-m* kin lover. Lit: he who loves his kinsmen

Toolmoon *name-f* beautiful, good, honest, virtuous, courteous

Toonno *nickname-m* Tunna (nicknamed by the Tunna fish)

Toosan *name-f* straight, direct; correct. Syn: Toosane

Toosane *name-m* straight, direct; correct. Syn: Toosan

Tooxan *nickname-f* curved, bent, arched. Cf: Godane. Syn: Tooxow

Tooxey *nickname-f* curved, bent, arched. Cf: Godane. Syn: Tooxow

Tooxow *nickname-m* curved, bent, arched. Cf: Godane. Syn: Tooxan
Tooyo *nickname-m* to ask questions, inquire, seek information. Lit: he who asks questions all the time
Tubeec[147] *nickname-m* sweet-voiced
Tufaax *name-f* apple
Tukaale[148] *nickname; name-m* crow, blackbird, raven. Lit: dark in color
Tumaal *nickname-m* blacksmith
Tuse *nickname-m* indicator; he who shows the right path
Tusmeeya *name-f* she who guides and indicates the good
Tusmo *name-unisex* post, fixed ~ assigned place; index, content; guidance

U

Ubax *name-f* flower; flowers. Syn: Ubaxo
Ubaxle *name-m* flower, flowers
Ubaxo *name-f* flower; flowers. Syn: Ubax
Ubbolacag *nickname; name-f* prosperous; rich
Udgoon *name-f* fragrant; aromatic; scent. Cf. Carfoon
Ugaar *nickname; name-m* prey, hunt; wild game
Ugaaryahan *nickname name-m* hunter of wild game
Ugaas *name-m* chief; king; sultan; boss
Ugaaso *name-f* queen; boss; princess
Ugbaad *name-f* virgin soil; unplowed land-- same as something fertile
Ujaajeen *name-m* to cry out; yeller, yelper, screamer, screecher, squealer. Cf: Cabaade, Wacwacle
Umal *nickname-unisex* wrath, anger, rage
Ummad *nickname-m* community, people, nation. Lit: a very social and manageable person
Ururshe *nickname-m* collector, compiler; responsible care-giver
Ursad *name-m* to smell or sniff. Lit: first born girl after a long

---

[147] Maxamed Suleymaan **Tubeec** (a very popular & golden-voiced Somali male singer)
[148] Maxamuud **Tukaale** Cismaan (well-known poet & playwright)

period of time of childlessness. Syn: Ursi
Ursi *name-f* to smell or sniff. Lit: first born-girl after a long period of time without having a child. Syn: Ursad
Uurdoox *name-m* belly stabber; to disembowel. Cf: Kaariye, Kaarshe, Muuddey or Muunye
Uurkuraag *name-m* past due, overdue
Uurmilil *nickname-m* envious ~ selfish, egotist, egoist
Uurweyne *nickname-m* bellie; dropsier

W

Waabberi *name-m* sunrise. Lit: one born in early morning
Wadaarre *name-m* masonary
Waadhowr *name-m* dawn-waiter. Lit: he who born at dawn
Waaqdoor *name-unisex* sky sky God's choice
Waaqmahadle *name-m* thanks to sky God
Waasuge[149] *name-m* dawn-waiter. Lit: he who born at dawn
Wabxiya *name-f* satisfaction, satisfying
Wabxiye *name-m* satisfaction, satisfying
Wacan *name-f* excellent, superb, very good
Wacayeen *name-m* blessed
Wacays *name-m* blessing
Wacaysle *name-m* the blessed
Wacdaan *name-m* help seeker
Wacwacle *name-m* to cry out; yeller, screamer, screecher, squealer, yelper. Cf: Cabaade, Ujaajeen
Wadaarre *nickname; name-m* mason; skilled
Wadalmoge *nickname-m* mindful; wise
Walaal *name-m* brother; darling; dear one
Walaalyabar *name-m* he who provides gifts to his wedding brother; the one born while his brother or sister is wedding-- as a gift from God (Walaal = brother or sister; yabar = wedding present)
Walax *nickname-m* fat, full, well fed
Walhad *nickname-m* vibrate, sway; swinger
Wali *name-f* Saint (Arb)
Wanaag *name-f* goodness, kindness, mercy; nice, excellent

---

[149] Cabdulle Nuur **Waasuge** (high jump sportsman)

Wanaaje *name-m* perfecter; good-doer
Waqantiile *nickname; name-m* warrior; tough; fighter
Waranhaye *name-m* brave; blessed; protector
Warantoble *name-m* warrior; tough; fighter; brave
Warcadde *name-m* trustworthy; articulate; truthful
Wardheer *name-f* famous, well-known; celebrated
Wardheere *name-m* famous, well-known; celebrated
Wardoox *nickname; name-m* news confirmer; articulated
Warfaa *name-m* catapult, restless; slinger, hurler; thrower. Cf: Marraaxaan, Marreexaan, Marriixaan
Warfog *name-f* famous, well-known; celebrated
Warla' *name-f* innocent
Warmoog *name-f; nickname-f* uninformed, unaware, innocent. Syn: Warmooge
Warmooge *name-m; nickname-m* uninformed, unaware, innocent. Syn: Warmoog
Warroon *name-f* good news; one who brings good news
Warsame *name-m* good news; one who brings good news
Warsan *name-f* good news; one who brings good news
Warsangeli *nickname-m* conveyer of good news; good news conveyer
Warwaaq *name-m* sky God's message or news
Warwaaqjecel *name-m* lover of sky God's word
Warwaaqsame *name-m* (war = news; Waaq = sky God; same = good) Good news from sky God
Warwaaqteen *name-m* good news from sky God
Wayteen *name-m* (exclamatory) to disappoint; disappointed; lamentor
Weheliye *name-m* companion, mate; company
Wiilo *nickname-f* boyish; she who dresses or behaves like boys; tomboy

X

Xaabeeya *name-f* fire-feeder
Xaabsade *nickname-m* he who gathers together ~ up for oneself or gathers things together. Lit: stronger; powerful. Syn: Xaabsey

Xaabsey *nickname-m* he who gathers together ~ up for oneself or gathers things together; lit: stronger; powerful. Syn: Xaabsade

Xaadsan *name-f* blemishless, smooth

Xaali *name-f* sweet; holy

Xaange[150] *name-m* fatty; well-rounded

Xaashi *name-m* paper. Lit: extremely light-skinned

Xaayow *name-m* whittishr; white flower. Cf: Xay, tish

Xabbad[151] *nickname; name-m* piece, one unit of something; single, solo, sole; bullet, cartridge; grain, seed, bead; sprinter. Cf: Rasaas

Xabeeb *nickname-m* hoarseness

Xaddi *name-m* decoration; decorator. Syn: Xaddiyo, Xiddo

Xaddiyo *name-f* decoration; decorator. Syn: Xaddi, Xiddo

Xafan *name-f* chopped, slashed

Xafane *name-m* chopped, slashed

Xagar *name-m* tree type specie

Xajiijle *name-m* clever, very active

Xalaawi *name-f* sweet cake (made from cornstarch, sugar, nutmeg and ghee or oil). Lit: sweetie. Cf: Xalwo

Xalan *name-f* clean, cleansed; pure. Cf: Xalane

Xalane *name-m* clean, cleansed; pure. Cf: Xalan

Xalwo *name-f* sweet cake (made from cornstarch, sugar, nutmeg and ghee or oil). Lit: sweetie. Cf: Xalaawi

Xamaro *name-f* chestnut ~ dark red color

Xamarre *name-m* chestnut ~ dark red color

Xamdulle *name-m* be grateful to; gratitude, gratefulness, thanks

Xanaf *nickname-m* roughness, harshness. Lit: troublesome

Xanaftire *name-m* conciliator, mediator

Xaraare *name-m* bitter taste; bitterness; acrid; sour. Lit: he whose enemy grieved at his birth while his parents and kinsmen were over-joyed

Xarbi[152] *name-m* to make war, fight, do battle. Lit: someone who

---

[150] Axmed Cartan **Xaange** (well-versed Somali literature collector and translator who authored a number of books)
[151] **Xabbad** Colaad Rasaas (Djiboutian singer)

was born during a memorable battle (Arb)

Xarfe *nickname-m* cooler; cooling. Lit: very patient one

Xarle *name-m* one with a distinguishing birthmark

Xarrago[153] *nickname-m* elegance, finery, splendor; refinement, pride. Cf: Mardaadi, Maruudi, Jooqle

Xareed *name-m* rainwater; sweet as rainwater; the one whose parents felt happiness upon his normal birth. Syn: Xareedo

Xareedo[154] *name-f* rainwater; sweet as rainwater; the one whose parents felt happiness upon her normal birth. Syn: Xareed

Xariir *name-m* diluted; silk (cloth ~ fabric); bleed, doctor an eye disease by bleeding. Lit: purity. Syn: Xariiro, Xariirre

Xariire *name-m* silk (cloth ~ fabric); bleed, doctor an eye disease by bleeding . Lit: purity. Syn: Xariir, Xariiro

Xariiro *name-f* silk (cloth ~ fabric); bleed, doctor an eye disease by bleeding. Lit: purity. Syn: Xariir, Xariirre

Xarle *name-m* decorater, carver, sculptor, etcher

Xarriiq *nickname; name-m* stripe

Xashan *name-f* elegant; husked

Xashane *name-m* elegant; husked

Xawaadle *nickname; name-m* jugular vein; throat

Xawse *nickname-m* mixed; colored

Xay *nickname; name-f* whittish; white flower. Cf: Xaayow, Xayle

Xaycad *name-f* bright white in color; white-maned

Xayndaan *name-m* circular fence, enclosure. Lit: protector; defense

Xaydar[155] *nickname; name-m* fine; soft haired. Syn: Yalax, Yalaxow, Yoolax

Xayd *nickname-m* lift ~ tucks up (one's clothing). Lit: ready for action

Xayeesi[156] *nickname-m* thinnes, slimness; thin ~ skinny person

Xayle *nickname; name-m* whittish; white flower. Cf: Xaayow, Xay

---

[152] Maxamuud **Xarbi** (independence fighter for former French Somaliland, now Republic of Djibouti. He died while under French custody)
[153] Cabdullaahi Cumar **Xarrago** (singer)
[154] **Xareedo** Ismaaciil Duniyo (legendary singer and actress)
[155] Siciid Mire **Xaydar** (singer)
[156] Maxamed Cabdalla Faarax **"Xayeesi"** (member of the 13th founders of the Somali Youth League (SYL)

Xayir *nickname; name-m* delay, detain, block. Lit: he who blocks the birthing pathway at the time of delivery
Xaynoosh[157] *nickname-m* hairy
Xiddeeye *name-m* decorator; ornamentor
Xiddo *name-f name-f* decorator. Syn: Xaddi, Xaddiyo
Xiddig *name-m* star. Syn: Xidigo
Xiddigo *name-f* star. Syn: Xidig
Xiirane *nickname-m* shaved, bolded
Xiireey *nickname-m* shaved, shaven
Xiis *name-m* current (of water ~ wind); high tide; interest, desire
Xiisaan *name-f* sash, cummerbund (Arb)
Xildiid *name-m* honorable behavior; juice ~ gum of a certain plant, used medicinally (Arb). Lit: blessed person
Ximyar *name-m* beautiful; string, thread. Lit: proportional; small-framed. Cf: Dhudi
Xinbil *name-m* promoter; beautifier; spite-healer. Cf: Xinbilo
Xinbilo *name-f* promoter; beautifier; spite-healer. Cf: Xinbil
Xintira *name-f* spite-eraser, hostility eliminator
Xintire *name-m* spite-eraser, hostility eliminator
Xirsi *name-m* amulet; charm; blessed. Cf: Xirsiyo
Xirsiyo *name-f* amulet; charm; blessed. Cf: Xirsi
Xoday *nickname; name-m* medicinal; medicinal herb sp.
Xoogsato *name-f* work-force, worker, proletariat
Xoosh *nickname; name-m* gray ~ light-colored skin/hair
Xooshow *nickname; name-m* gray~light-colored skin/hair
Xorriyo *name-f* freedom, indepencence; independent
Xubbi *name-f* love (Arb)
Xuddubey name-m explainer, lecturer; analyzer, definer
Xujaale *nickname; name-m* riddler; task-master or one who poses a difficult question or problem; harasser-- Lit: a tough or difficult person to deal with
Xulbado *name-f* curative, plant sp., plant with edible fruit, used Medicinally. Lit: blessed. Cf: Xildiid
Xubeer *nickname; name-m* poor, starved. Cf: Cayr
Xukun *nickname; name-unisex* rule, command; verdict, judgement. Lit: he/she who rules

---

[157] Cabdiraxmaan **Xaynoosh** (comedian & bass-guitarist)

Xurmo *name-f* honor, respect; favor, grace (Arb)
Xuubey *nickname; name-m* sloughed skin; fetal membrane
Xuudi *nickname; name-m* whale
Xuur *nickname-m* exhaustion. Lit: a weak and vulnerable person
Xuuxuule *nickname; name-m* (onomatopoeic). Lit: the one who was born with a whooping cough
Xuuxaaye *nickname-m* (onomatopoeic) the one who growled or made guttural sounds at birth

Y

Yaabur *name-m* dry-skinned
Yabar *name-m* gift; generousity; hypnotize; exorcise
Yabar-cadde *name-m* proven exorcism; hypnotizer; generous; gifter; articulated
Yabarow *name-m* gifter; exorcizer; evil eye healer; generous
Yabarre *nickname-m* exorciser; hypnotizer; evil eye healer; gifter; generous
Yalax nickname; *name-m* fine; soft haired. Syn: Yalaxow, Yoolax
Yalaxow *nickname; name-m* fine; soft haired. Syn: Yalax, Yoolax
Yarafle *nickname-m* marauder
Yeey[158] *nickname-m* wolf; wild dog; jackal
Yogol *name-m* tall and dark
Yoolax *nickname; name-m* fine; soft haired. Syn: Yalax, Yalaxow
Yurub *name-f* Europe. Lit: very light-skinned; white

õõõ

---

[158] Colonel Cabdullaahi Yuusuf **Yeey** (president of the transitional federal government of Somalia)

Chapter II
Names of Arabic and Islamic Root

You who believe let no man deride another who may be better than he, let no woman deride another who may be better than she. Neither defames one another, nor insults one another by bad nicknames. It is bad to use an abusive name instead of one you can believe in. Those who do not turn away from such a practice are wrongdoers.
In the Qur'an, Al-Hujuraat, Sura 49 verse 11.

A

Aaden *name-m* man, human being, earth; Prophet in the holy Qur'an
Aamina[159] *name-f* trustworthy, loyal, dependable, secure, faithful
Aasiya *name-f* firm, powerful, a good person, comforting, consoling; wife of Pharoah
Abraar *name-f* devoted to God
Abuubakar *name-m* father of the reliable one; the first Caliph of Islam (623-624)
Afrax *name-m* happier, happiest
Almaas *name-unisex* diamond
Amaal *name-f* hopes, aspirations
Amaan *name-m* trust, safe, peace, security
Amaana *nam-f* trust, safe, peace, security
Amal *name-f* hope, aspiration
Ammiin[160] *name-m* praiseworthy
Amiir *name-m* prince, ruler, leader
Amiira *name-f* princess, ruler, leader
Ammuun *name-f* trustworthy
Anas *name-m* very sociable

---

[159] **Aamina** Cabdullaahi (Somali female singer)
[160] **Ammiin** Caamir (well-known Somali artist)

Anisa *name-f* good companion, friendly
Ansaari *name-m* my helper
Anwar *name-m* rays of light, lightest, bright, lustre
Anwaar *name-f* rays of light, lightest, bright, blossoms, lustre
Asad *name-m* lion, strong
Ashraf *name-m* most honorable, most noble, superior
Ashwaaq *name-f* love, affectionate
Asiili *name-f* of good lineage
Asma *name-f* most exalted
Aswad *name-m* black, master
Axmed[161] *name-m* more, most grateful, praiseworthy
Axmed-wardi *name-m* the most graceful rose
Ayuub *name-m* persecuted, penitent (Job); Prophet in the holy Qur'an
Azhar *name-m* clearer, more evident
Azhaar *name-f* flowers

B

Basma *name-f* smiling
Badar *name-m* full moon
Badri *name-m* early, resembling full moon
Badriya *name-f* early, resembling full moon
Badrudiin *name-m* moon of the faith
Bakar *name-m* young camel, reliable, first born
Balqiisa *name-f* female ruler of Sheba
Bariir *name-m* faithful
Bashaar *name-m* messenger of good news, bringer of many glad tidings
Bashiir[162] *name-m* predictor, forerunner, bringer of glad tidings
Bashiira *name-f* predictor, forerunner, bringer of glad tidings
Batuulo *name-f* chaste, virgin
Baxar *name-m* Ocean; clever; dangerous man

---

[161] Maxamed **Axmed** Cali (education pioneer of British Somaliland or Northern Somalia')
[162] Sheekh **Bashiir** & **Bashiir** Salaad Xirsi (independence-minded mullah in Northern Somalia; Somali playwright & poet, respectively)

Bayaan *name-m* clear, evident
Bilaal *name-m* dampness of rain, moisture, freshness. Lit: that which satisfies thirst
Bishaara *name-f* good news, predictor of good news, good tidings
Burhaan *name-m* proof
Burhaanudiin *name-m* proof (evidence) of the faith
Bushra *name-f* announcer of good news, joyful, good omen; happiness
Busur *name-f* unripe dates; star; height

C

Caadil *name-m* just, one who acts justly
Caadila *name-f* just, one who acts justly
Caafiya *name-m* health; one who heals
Caalim[163] *name-m* learned, educated
Caaliya *name-f* exalted, sublime, high, excellent
Caamir *name-m* prosperous
Caaqil *name-m* sensible; wise
Caaqila *name-f* wife, spouse; the best of the pick
Caasha *name-f* alive, living; prosperous
Cabbaas *name-m* lion, stern
Cabdalla *name-m* God's servant
Cabdi *name-m* servant
Cabdille *name-m* God's servant. Cf. Cabdalla
Cabdow *name-m* servant. Cf. Cabdi
Cabdulatiif *name-m* servant of the Gentle One
Cabdulaxad *name-m* servant of the One
Cabdulbaasid *name-m* servant of the Receiver
Cabdulbashiir *name-m* servant of the Messenger
Cabdulcaadil *name-m* servant of the Just One
Cabdulcaali *name-m* servant of the Most High
Cabdulcaziiz *name-m* servant of the Almighty
Cabdulfataax *name-m* servant of the Opener

---

[163] Professor **Caalim** (Somali mathematics professor at the University of Lafoole, Somalia)

Cabdulkariim *name-m* servant of the Generous
Cabdulkhaaliq *name-m* servant of the Creator
Cabdullaahi[164] *name-m* God's servant
Cabdulmaalik *name-m* servant of the King
Cabdulmajeed *name-m* servant of the Exalted
Cabdulnuur *name-m* servant of the Light
Cabdulqaadir[165] *name-m* servant of the Capable
Cabdulqafaar *name-m* servant of the Forgiver
Cabdulqani *name-m* servant of the Rich
Cabdulqawi *name-m* servant of the Strong
Cabdulra'uuf *name-m* servant of the Merciful
Cabdulrashiid *name-m* servant of the Intelligent
Cabdulrasuul *name-m* servant of the Messenger
Cabdulraxiim *name-m* servant of the Compassionate
Cabdulraxmaan *name-m* servant of the Merciful
Cabdulrisaaq[166] *name-m* servant of the Provider
Cabdulsamad *name-m* servant of the Eternal
Cabdulshakuur *name-m* servant of the Grateful
Cabdulsitaar *name-m* servant of the Protector
Cabdulsuldaan *name-m* servant of the Ruler
Cabdultawaab *name-m* servant of the Forgiver
Cabdultayaar *name-m* servant of the Ready
Cabdulwaaxid *name-m* servant of the Unique
Cabdulwadduud *name-m* servant of the Loving
Cabdulwahaab *name-m* servant of the Giver
Cabdulwakiil *name-m* servant of the Guardian
Cabdulweli *name-m* servant of the Protector
Cabdulxakiim *name-m* servant of the Wise
Cabdulxaliim *name-m* servant of the Gentle
Cabdulxamiid *name-m* servant of the Praiseworthy
Cabiid *name-m* devout

---

[164] **Cabdullaahi** Ciise Maxamuud (first prime minister of Italian Somaliland during the Trusteeship 1956-1960)
[165] **Cabdulqaadir** Xirsi Siyaad 'Yam-Yam' (leading poet of the Somali peninsula in the second half of the twentieth century who died in a car accident in Columbus, Ohio on October 21, 2005)
[166] **Cabdulrisaaq** Xaaji Xuseen (second prime minister of the Somali Republic 1964-1967)

Cabla *name-f* wild rose, perfectly formed
Cafiif *name-m* virtuous, pure, chaste, modest
Cafiifa *name-f* virtuous, pure, chaste, modest
Calaawi *name-f* the great
Cali[167] *name-m* exalted, high, lofty; the fourth Caliph of Islam (656-661) Cf: Caliyow
Cammaar *name-m* one who is a builder, long lived, or preserver of life
Cammaari *name-m* one who is builder, long lived, or preserver of life
Cantar *name-m* blue flies, brave, hero
Caaqil *name-m* wise
Cariif *name-m* knowledgeable, cognizant, acquainted
Cariifa *name-f* knowledgeable, cognizant, acquainted
Cawad *name-m* reward, compensation
Caziiz *name-m* precious, glorious, powerful, dear
Caziiza *name-f* precious, glorious, powerful, dear
Cibaado *name-f* worshipful; also Cabidah
Ciise *name-m* saviour; Jesus; Prophet in the holy Qur'an
Cimraan *name-m* prosperity, be long lived
Cizadiin *name-m* the power of the faith
Cubayd *name-m* young worshipper, servant of God
Cubayda *name-f* young worshipper, servant of God. Cf. Cibadah or Cibaado
Cudaay *name-m* one who runs fast; 'Uday
Cumar *name-m* lifetime, longevity, ageless; the second Caliph of Islam (634-644)
Cuqayl *name-m* wise, intelligent
Cusaama *name-m* lion, brave
Cismaan[168] *name-m* wealthy; young reptile, snake; the third Caliph of Islam (644-656)

---

[167] **Cali** Cilmi Af-yare (well-known Somali poet)
[168] **Cismaan** Yuusuf Keenadiid (Somali poet and founder of the first ever written native Somali script known as **Cismaaniya**)

D

Daakir *name-m* one who remembers God frequently
Daa'uud *name-m* beloved; David; Prophet in the holy Qur'an
Daahir *name-m* clean
Daliila *name-f* proof
Dalxa[169] *name-m* name of a place, acacia tree
Darwiish *name-m* religious, pious; Dervish
Dayib *name-m* good, pure, sinless
Diima *name-f* cloud which carries rain
Diina *name-f* religious
Ducaa *name-f* prayer, invocation of God
Duniyo *name-f* world, earth

F

Faadil *name-m* victorious, virtuous, superior, honorable; abundance
Faadila *name-f* victorious, virtuous, superior, honorable; abundance
Fadiil *name-m* virtuous, outstanding; abundance
Fadiila *name-f* virtuous, outstanding; abundance
Faaduma *name-f* intelligent; weaning
Faahim *name-m* intelligent, learned
Faa'iz *name-m* victorious, triumphant; success
Faa'iza *name-f* victorious, triumphant; success
Faakhir *name-m* excellent, magnificent, proud, outstanding
Faakhira *name-f* excellent, magnificent, proud, outstanding
Faarax *name-m* cheerful; happiness, joy
Faaruuq *name-m* he who distinguishes truth from falsehood, clarifier
Faatix *name-m* conqueror
Fadal *name-m* favor; surplus
Fahad *name-m* panther, lynx; powerful

---

[169] Maxamed Cumar **Dalxa** (first vice deputy of the transitional federal parliament of Somalia was a former lacturer at the faculty of languages at Somalia's National University)

Fahiim *name-m* learned
Fahiima *name-f* learned
Fahma *name-f* learned
Fakhrudiin *name-m* the glory of the faith
Falaax *name-m* farmer
Fannaan *nickname; name-m* artist; performer
F aarax *name-m* relief, freedom from grief
Farax *name-f* happiness, Joy, cheerfulness
Fardowsa *name-f* a level of paradise mentioned in the Q'uran
Farduus *name-f* paradise
Fariid *name-m* unique, precious, rare
Fariida *name-f* unique, precious, rare
Fariixa *name-f* joyful
Farxaan *name-f* happy
Farxiya *name-f* joyful
Fasiixa *name-m* eloquent
Fatima *name-f* intelligent, weaning
Fatma *name-f* intelligent, weaning
Fatxi *name-m* triumph; to conquer
Fatxiya *name-f* triumph, to conquer
Fatuun *name-f* fascination
Fawzi *name-m* to achieve success; succesful
Fawziya *name-f* to achieve success; successful
Fayruus *name-f* turquoise
Faysal[170] *name-m* arbitrator, decisive; criterion
Firyaal *name-f* extraordinary
Fu'aad *name-m* heart
Furqaan *name-m* proof, evidence, clarity

G

Guhaad *name-m* striver; to strive

---

[170] **Faysal** Cumar Mushteeg (Somali singer)

H

Haajira *name-f* exiled, Prophet Ibrahim's wife; Hajar
Haaruun *name-m* enlightened, lofty; Aaron-- Prophet in the holy Qur'an
Haashim *name-f* respectful
Hadi *name-m* leader, guide
Hadiya *name-f* gift
Hana *name-f* happiness, peace of mind, bliss
Hanan *name-f* love, compassion
Haybe *name-m* esteem; one who has esteem
Hibo *name-f* gift, present
Hilaal *name-m* crescent, new moon
Hinda *name-f* a large flock of camels; hence wealth
Huda *name-f* guidance, direction, right course
Huud *name-m* repenting; Prophet in the holy Qur'an

I

Ibraahim[171] *name-m* father of many nations; Abraham, prophet in the holy Qur'an. Cf: Ibrow
Ibtisaam *name-f* smile
Idiris *name-m* teacher; Enoch, Prophet in the holy Qur'an
Iimaan[172] *name-unisex* faith, compassion
Ikhlaas *name-f* devotion; sincere, pure, loyal, constant
Ikraam *name-f* hospitality, respect
Ilhaam *name-f* inspiration, intuition
Ilhaan *name-f* inspiration, intuition
Ilyaas *name-m* Allah is God; Elijah, Prophet in the holy Qur'an
Imaam *nickname-m* leader
Intisaar *name-f* victory; victorious, triumph
Ismaaciil[173] *name-m* Allah heard; Ismael, prophet in the holy

---

[171] Maxamed **Ibraahim** Warsame 'Hadraawi' (very popular & prominent Somali poet)
[172] **Iimaan** Cabdulmajiid (Somali-born model)

Qur'an
Israa *name-f* nocturnal journey, night journey of Prophet Muhammad from Mekka to Jerusalem
Isxaaq *name-m* he laughed; Isaac; Prophet in the holy Qur'an
Ismahaan *name-f* most exalted, ruler
Ixsaan *name-unisex* beneficence, charity, kindness; courteous, doing good
Iyaad *name-m* pigeon

J

Jaabir *name-m* brave; bonesetter, repairer, counselor, comforter
Jacfar *name-m* Small River, rivulet, little creek
Jamaal *name-m* handsome, graceful
Jamaaludiin *name-m* the glory of the faith
Jamiil *name-m* handsome, graceful, good looking, charming
Jamiila *name-f* beautiful, pretty, graceful, charming
Jawhar *name-m* gem, jewel
Jawhara *name-f* gem, jewel
Jibriil *name-m* servant of God or Cabdullaah; biblical Gabriel; angel of God
Jihaad *name-m* to exert effort, struggle; religious struggle; striving for the sake of or in the service of God
Jilani *name-m* land with hard soil; lit: he who was born in a land with hard soil. Cf: Dhooddi, Jeylaani
Joohaar *name-m* gem, jewel
Jookha *name-f* embroidered brocade
Juweyriya *name-f* damask rose

K

Kaafiya *name-f* self-sufficient
Kaamil *name-m* perfection, completed
Kaamila *name-f* perfection, completed

---

[173] Maxamuud **Ismaaciil** Xudeydi 'Somali song writer, lyricist & musician who plays the **Oud** or **Kaban**)

Kaatiba *name-f* writer
Kaltuun *name-f* beautiful face
Kamaal *name-m* perfection
Kamaaludiin *name-m* the perfection of the faith
Kariim *name-m* generous, noble
Kariima *name-f* generous, noble
Kawsar *name-f* lady; river in heaven; star; abundance; river in paradise
Khaalid *name-m* friend; lasting; eternal
Khadar *name-m* green; fertility
Khadiija *name-f* great; Prophet Muhammad's first wife
Khadra *name-f* green, fertility
Khalaf *name-m* descendant, successor
Khaliida *name-f* immortal, survinving
Khaliif[174] *name-m* vice-regent, successor
Khaliil *name-m* sincere; friend
Khaliila *name-f* sincere; friend
Khamiis[175] *name-m* one born on Thursday
Khayrre *name-m* beneficent, good
Khayriya *name-f* charitable; good

L

Latiif *name-m* gentle, delicate, sensitive, kind, courteous
Latiifa *name-f* gentle, delicate, sensitive, kind, courteous
Leyla *name-f* night; sweetheart
Liin *name-m* graceful, tender
Liima *name-f* graceful, tender
Lubna *name-f* resin, precious, flexible
Ludfiya *name-f* kind, kindness; gentle
Luqmaan *name-m* wise; Prophet in the holy Qur'an
Luud *name-m* hidden; Lut; Prophet in the holy Qur'an
Luula *name-f* pearl, jewel

---

[174] **Khaliif** Sheekh Maxamuud (well-versed Somali poet 1960-1983)
[175] Aweys **Khamiis** Maputo (Somali singer & lyricist)

M

Maahir *name-m* clever, expert, skillful
Maahira *name-f* clever, expert, skillful
Maajida *name-f* glorious, praise-worthy
Macallin *nickname; name-m* teacher
Macruuf *name-m* well known; good
Madiina *name-f* the holy city of Medina
Mahdi *name-m* leader, guide, reformer, rightly-guided, follower of the true faith
Majiid *name-m* honorable, glorious
Maki *name-m* Mecca
Malayka *name-f* ruler, queen, angel
Maleyka *name-f* ruler, queen, angel
Maliika *name-f* ruler, queen, angel
Maliixa *name-f* beautiful, pleasant
Mannaan *name-m* bountiful, generous
Mansuur *name-m* protected, victorious, triumphant
Maryan[176] *name-f* blessed, honorable, noble; biblical Mary; mother of Prophet Issa or biblical Jesus
Marzuuq *name-m* blessed by Allah, prosperous
Masbal *name-f* aromatic tree; aromatic assense; graceful
Mascuud *name-m* fortunate, happy
Maslax *name-m* reformer, reconciler, pacifier
Mawliid *name-m* the day of the year marking the birth of Prophet Muhammad
Maxamed *name-m* honorable, praised, praise-worthy. Muhammad is regarded by Muslims as the last Prophet of Allah or God
Maxamuud[177] *name-m* honorable, praised, praise-worthy
Maymuun *name-f* blessed, happy, lucky, fortunate
Maymuuna *name-f* blessed, happy, lucky, fortunate
Maysara[178] *name-m* easiness, comfort
Mina *name-f* fortunate
Miski *name-f* musk

---

[176] **Maryan** Mursal Ciise (energetic & sweet-voiced singer)
[177] **Maxamuud** Cabdullaahi Singub (one of the most talented Somali playwrights & poets)
[178] Macallin **Maysara** (Somali guitarist)

Mubaarak *name-m* blessed
Mucammar *name-m* given or granted long life
Mujaahid *name-m* striver in the service of the faith
Mukhtaar *name-m* chosen
Mumtaas *name-f* distinguished
Muna *name-f* hope, wish, desire
Muniir *name-m* bright, brilliant, counselor, radiant
Muniira *name-f* bright, brilliant, counselor, radiant
Muraad *name-m* desired purpose; intention, want
Mursal *name-m* righteous, rightly-guarded
Murtada *name-m* contented, pleased
Muslim *name-m* one who submits to Allah's will; faithful
Muslima *name-f* one who submits to Allah's will; faithful
Mustafa *name-m* chosen, selected
Muumin[179] *name-m* faithful; true believe
Muumina *name-f* faithful; true believer
Muuse *name-m* drawing out, extracting from water; Moses, prophet in the holy Qur'an
Muxyadiin *name-m* revivalist, the sustainer of the faith
Muxsin *name-m* beneficent, charitable
Muxubo *name-f* beloved

N

Naada *name-f* generosity, dew
Naadir *name-m* rare, precious
Naadiya *name-f* lively, pretty; announcement
Naafic *name-m* useful
Naaji[180] *name-m* confident, friendly, affectionate, safe; survivor
Naasir *name-m* supporter, helper, triumphed, defender;
Nabiil *name-m* noble, proclaimed, honorable
Nabiila *name-f* noble, proclaimed, honorable
Naciim *name-m* comfortable, blessing, happiness

---

[179] Xasan Sheekh **Muumin** (Somali playwright, one of whose his best play is ***Shabeel Naagood*** "Leopard Among the Women" which was staged in 1968)
[180] Axmed **Naaji** Sacad (Somali song-writer, singer, musician & lyricist)

Naciima *name-f* comfortable, blessing, happiness
Nadiir *name-m* consecrated to God, rare, precious and unique
Nadiira *name-f* consecrated to God, rare, precious and unique
Nadwa *name-f* counsel; generosity
Nafisa *name-f* valuable, costly, precious
Nahla *name-f* a drink of water
Najax *name-unisex* success; safe, rescued, delivered
Najiib *name-m* noble, high-bred, excellent, outstanding
Najiiba *name-f* noble, high-bred, excellent, outstanding
Najla *name-f* the one who has beautiful eyes; wide eyes
Najam *name-m* star-like; astrologer
Najma *name-f* star-like; astrologer
Najmudiin *name-m* star of the faith
Naqma *name-f* selection; pure; clean and clear
Nasar *name-m* helper, protector, granter of victory
Nasri *name-m* victory
Nasiib *name-m* luck, lucky; noble; relative
Nasrullah *name-m* saved by God
Nawaal *name-f* benefit, gift, attainment
Nawaar *name-f* one who dislikes bad deeds
Naziir *name-m* leader, vanguard; equal-like, matching
Naziira *name-f* leader, vanguard; equal-like, matching
Nizaa *name-f* women; she that makes men to forget
Nizriin *name-f* a kind of aromatic plant
Nucmaan *name-unisex* a red plant; blessed, rosy-colored
Nuur *name-m* light; flower, blossom
Nuura[181] *name-f* shining stone; flower, blossom
Nuuraani *name-m* the light
Nuuriya *name-f* luminous
Nuurudiin[182] *name-m* the light of the faith
Nuux *name-m* to sway; howl; rest; Noah: Prophet in the holy Qur'an
Nuuxa *name-f* wisdom, prudence

---

[181] Hibo **Nuura** (Somali female singer)
[182] **Nuurudiin** Faarax (internationally acclaimed Somali-born novelist who won the Pulitzer Price in 2001)

Q

Qaadi[183] *nickname; name-m* judge
Qaali *name-f* valuable, dear, beloved, expensive
Qaalib *name-m* victor; victorious, overcoming, conquering, dominant, successful
Qaaliba *name-f* victor; victorious, overcoming, conquering, dominant, successful
Qaasim[184] *name-m* self-controlled; well-tempered, cool, patient, just; divider, distributor
Qaasima *name-f* self-controlled, well-tempered, cool, patient, just; divider, distributor
Qaazi *name-m* conqueror. Cf. Ghaazi
Qamar[185] *name-f* full moon
Qaniima *name-f* great benefit
Qaniya *name-f* rich; contented
Qaws *name-m* succor, help. Cf. Ghawth
Qays[186] *name-m* firm
Qudub *name-m* leader. Cf. Qutb
Qudsiya *name-f* glorious; sacred

R

Raabi *name-m* spring; pleasant
Raani *name-m* gazing; gaze; resonate
Raaniya *name-f* gazing; gaze; resonate
Raaqiya *name-f* superior
Raawiya *name-f* entertainer, story-teller, narrator
Rabiica *name-f* iron helmet, strong; fourth
Rabiixa *name-f* winner
Rafiiq *name-m* companion, friend, ally

---

[183] Sheekh Cabdulraxmaan Sheekh Nuur **Qaadi** (inventor of Borama script)
[184] Axmed Saalax **Qaasim** (Somali singer, musician & lyricist)
[185] **Qamar** Cabdullaahi Harawo (Somali female folklore dancer who sings occasionally)
[186] Cabdi Aadan Xaad "**Qays**" (Somali playwright & poet)

Rafiiqa *name-f* companion, friend, ally
Rajaa *name-f* hope
Rajeeya *name-f* hoping; full of hope
Ramla *name-f* divination; predictor of the future
Ramzi *name-m* symbolic; in code, coded
Rashaad *name-m* integrity of conduct; reason, good sense; majurity, wisdom
Rashiid *name-m* wise, righteous, rightly-guided; intelligent, sensible
Rashiida *name-f* wise, righteous, rightly-guided; intelligent, sensible
Raxiima *name-f* merciful, kind, compassionate
Raxma *name-f* merciful, kind, compassionate
Ra'uuf *name-m* merciful; gentle
Rayaax *name-f* aroma, fragrance
Ridwaan *name-m* good-will, forgiveness; satisfaction, consent
Ridwaana *name-f* contented
Ruqiya *name-f* superior
Rushdi *name-m* mature, wise
Ruwayd *name-m* walking gently
Ruwayda *name-f* walking gently
Ruuxi *name-unisex* of the spirit; spiritual

S

Saabir *name-m* patient; endurance
Saabira *name-f* patient; endurance
Saadaad *name-unisex* the right thing to do; lucky hand. Cf: Sadat
Saadiq *name-m* friend, truthful, sincere
Saadiqa *name-f* friend, truthful, sincere
Saafi *name-m* pure, sincere, clear
Saajida *name-f* worshiper
Saalax[187] *name-m* goodness; righteousness
Saalim *name-m* safe, peaceable; healthy, secure

---

[187] Siciid **Saalax** Axmed (Somali playwright, song writer, film maker, poet, educator & literary scholar)

Saalima *name-f* safe, peaceable; healthy, secure
Saalix *name-m* honest, virtuous, upright, pious; goodness. Cf: Saalih; Prophet in the holy Qur'an
Saalixa *name-f* honest, virtuous, upright, pious
Saamiya *name-f* exalted, elevated, lofty; to hear; listener
Saara *name-f* joyful; Prophet Ibrahim's wife
Saariya *name-f* night clouds; noble
Saba *name-f* eastern wind, Zephyr
Sabaax *name-f* morning; pleasant
Sabri *name-m* of patience; perseverance
Sabriin *name-f* patient
Sabriye *name-m* patient
Sacad *name-m* happy; good luck
Sacdiya *name-f* helper
Sacfaraan *name-f* saffron
Saciid *name-m* happiness
Saciida *name-f* happiness
Sadiiq *name-m* trustworthy, friend; one who keeps his word; righteousness
Sadiiqa *name-f* trustworthy, friend; one who keeps her word; righteousness
Safa *name-f* purity, serenity, clarity
Safiya *name-f* immaculate, pure, serene; best friend
Sahiira *name-f* awake, vigilant
Sahal *name-m* easy to deal with; easy-goer
Sahla *name-f* easy to deal with; easy-goer
Sakiina *name-f* tranquility, calmness
Salma *name-f* peaceful, safe, secure, healthy, wholesome
Salmaan *name-m* peaceful, safe, secure, healthy, wholesome (name of the first Persian to embrace Islam)
Salwa *name-f* consolation; quail (symbol of prophecy); generosity
Samiir *name-m* companion, entertainer, pleasant, patient, conversant
Samiira *name-f* companion, entertainer, pleasant, patient, conversant
Saruur *name-m* happy
Sayid *nickname; name-m* chief, master
Sayida *name-f* lady, chief, mistress

Shaadiya *name-f* praise, commend, exert; singer
Shaafi *name-m* healer, mediator
Shaafici *name-m* healer, mediator
Shaafiya *name-f* healer, mediator
Shaahid *name-m* witness; one who upholds the faith
Shaahida *name-f* witness; one who upholds the faith
Shaakir *name-m* thankful, grateful
Shaakira *name-f* thankful, grateful
Shabaaba *name-f* young lady
Shafiica *name-f* mediator
Shafiiqa *name-f* kind, compassionate
Shahrazad *name-f* princess
Shakiib *name-m* present, gift, reward
Shakuur *name-m* Grateful
Shamaal *name-m* wind that comes from the North
Shamis *name-f* sun, sunlight
Shamsa *name-f* sun, sunlight
Shamso *name-f* sun, sunlight
Shamsudiin *name-m* the sun of the faith
Shariif *name-m* noble, honorable; descendant of Prophet Muhammad
Shariifo *name-f* noble, honorable; descendant of Prophet Muhammad
Shifaa *name-f* healing
Sheekh[188] *nickname-m* leader, elderly; learned
Shucayb *name-m* abundance, excellence; popular, one who branches out. Prophet in the holy Qur'an
Shukri *name-unisex* to be grateful; thankful for
Sihaam *name-f* participation; arrows
Siidi *name-m* master
Siraaj *name-m* lighted torch
Siti *name-f* lady
Sucaad *name-f* happy, good fortune
Suhayb *name-m* red-haired (name of the first Roman to embrace Islam)
Suhayl *name-m* constellation (canopus) Sirius, brightest star; easy

---

[188] **Sheekh** Aweys (Sufism Tarriqa leader in southern Somalia)

    to deal with, fluent, smooth, soft
Suhayla *name-f* constellation (canopus) Sirius, brightest star; easy to deal with, fluent, smooth, soft
Sukayna *name-f* calm, charming, likable
Suldaan *name-m* ruler, king
Suldaana *name-f* ruler, queen
Suleymaan *name-m* peace; Solomon, prophet in the holy Qur'an
Sumaya *name-f* good reputation, high rank; first martyr in Islam
Sundus *name-f* silk brocade
Sureya *name-f* sun; free of worries, happy
Suwayda *name-f* diminutive of black

T

Taabad *name-m* firm, constant, determined
Taaha *name-m* the two opening letters of 20th Surah of the Qur'an; it is said to be one of the names of Prophet Muhammad
Taahira *name-f* neat, pure, clean
Taamiya *name-f* impeccable
Taariq *name-m* visitor; piercing star
Taha *name-m* man, opening of 20th Surah of the Qur'an
Talaal *name-m* nice, admirable
Taalib *name-m* seeker of knowledge
Talxa *name-m* easy life
Taqi *name-m* God fearing, heedful of God
Taqiya *name-f* God fearing, heedful of God
Tasliima *name-f* salutation, peace
Tasmiina *name-f* precious
Tawfiiq *name-m* divine guidance, success granted by God
Tawfiiqa *name-f* divine guidance, success granted by God
Tawxiid *name-m* belief in one God
Tawxiida *name-f* belief in one God
Taysiir *name-m* facilitation; granted by God
Thaani[189] *name-m* second

---

[189] Ismaaciil Xuseen **Thaani** (Djiboutian journalist, literary scholar & politician)

Thaabit *name-m* steadfast, firm
Tufaaxo *name-f* apple

U

Ubax *name-f* flower; rose, blossom. Cf: Warda, Wardi
Um-Kaltuun *name-f* Kaltuun's mother, Prophet Muhammad's daughter
Uways[190] *name-m* name of a wolf
Uwaysa *name-f* bilberry, whortleberry

W

Waafiya *name-f* loyal, faithful, constant
Waaxid *name-m* unique, one, alone
Wahaab *name-m* giver
Wahaaj *name-m* brilliant, shining
Waliid *name-m* new born son; product
Waliida *name-f* new born daughter; product
Waliya *name-f* ruler
Warda *name-f* rose, blossom, flowers. Cf: Ubax
Wardi *name-m* rose, blossom, flowers. Cf: Ubax
Wardiya *name-f* rosy
Warqa *name-f* pigeon
Waxiid *name-m* unique, one, alone, indivisible
Waxiida *name-f* unique, one, alone, indivisible
Waziir *name-m* secretary, minister
Waziira *name-f* secretary, minister
Widaad *name-f* affectionate, gentle

X

Xaafid *name-m* preserver, memorizer
Xaajji *nickname-m* one who was on a pilgrimage
Xaamud *name-m* grateful, praise-worthy

---

[190] Sheekh **Uways** Maxamed (Somali-born mystic and reformer in East Africa who lived between 1847-1909)

Xaaris *name-m* protector, watchman
Xaawo[191] *name-f* Eve; warm air
Xabiib *name-m* beloved, dear one; darling
Xabiiba *name-f* beloved, dear one; darling
Xabiibullah *name-m* God's beloved
Xadi *name-m* divine ordinance
Xafsa *name-f* sound judgment
Xafza *name-f* cub, young lioness
Xakiim *name-m* sensible, wise, judge, gentle
Xakiima *name-f* sensible, wise, judge, gentle
Xaliima *name-f* fore-bearing
Xamdi *name-f* praise; gratitude
Xamiid *name-m* grateful, one who praises
Xamiida *name-f* grateful, one who praises
Xamza *name-m* in control; lion, strong
Xanaan *name-f* affectionate
Xanaf *name-m* true believer
Xaniif *name-m* pure, true believer, upright
Xaniifa *name-f* pure, true believer, upright
Xasan *name-m* good, handsome
Xasiina *name-f* beautiful
Xasna *name-f* beautiful, good
Xayaat *name-f* life
Xaydar *name-m* lion, strength
Xirsi *name-m* guard, amulet
Xuseen *name-m* good, handsome
Xusna *name-f* most beautiful, goodness
Xusni *name-m* most handsome, goodness

Y

Yaasir *name-m* wealthy, rich
Yaasiin[192] *name-m* principle; title of the 36th Sura in the Qur'an

---

[191] **Xaawo** Cusmaan Taako (female icon of Somalia's freedom fighters died in 1948)

Yaciish *name-m* he lives
Yacquub *name-m* repented, he who stepped back from wicked ways, he who follows; supplanter. Jacob, prophet in the holy Qur'an
Yamani *name-m* blessings; from Yemen
Yamiin *name-m* right hand, loyal, honest, blessed
Yamiina *name-f* right hand, loyal, honest, blessed
Yasiir *name-m* ease, gentle; prosperous
Yasmiin *name-f* Jasmine, flower
Yaxya *name-m* Allah is gracious, he lives. John, the Baptist; prophet in the holy Qur'an
Yoonis *name-m* dove; affection. Jonah, prophet in the holy Qur'an
Yumna *name-f* good fortune, wealth; right side
Yusra *name-f* ease and comfort, easiness, relief; well-to-do, wealthy
Yusur *name-f* she makes it easy, ease, relief; well-to-do, wealthy
Yusriya *name-f* most prosperous
Yuusuf *name-m* Allah will increase; Joseph, prophet in the holy Qur'an

Z

Zaahid *name-m* abstinent, ascetic
Zaarifa *name-f* elegant, witty
Zaciid *name-m* increased in oil; wisdom
Zahiir *name-m* radiant, bright, outstanding, flowery, shining; supporter
Zahiira *name-f* radiant, bright, outstanding, flowery, shining; supporter
Zahra[193] *name-f* beauty, flower, blossom
Zakariya *name-m* Allah remembered; Zachariah; prophet in the holy Qur'an
Zaki *name-m* virtuous, guiltless, intelligent, pure, sharp; growth

---

[192] **Yaasiin** Cismaan Keenadiid (Somali literary scholar who is the author of the first-ever written Somali to Somali dictionary, published in Muqdisho, Somalia in 1976)
[193] **Zahra** Siyaad & **Zahra** Axmed (Somali female singers)

Zakiya *name-f* virtuous, guiltless, intelligent, pure, sharp; growth
Zayid *name-m* increasing, growing
Zayn *name-f* beautiful, graceful
Zaynab[194] *name-f* beautyful, graceful, aromatic tree
Zaytuun *name-f* olive, guava
Ziyaad *name-m* super abundance
Zubayda *name-f* best part, cream, butter, delicate; a piece of butter; wife of Caliph Harun Al-Rashid
Zuhayr *name-m* Venus; blossom, radiant, shining
Zuhayra *name-f* Venus; blossom, radiant, shining
Zuhuur *name-f* flowers
Zuleekha *name-f* ahead, brilliant
Zulfa *name-m* he who likes to please

õõõ

---

[194] **Zaynab** Xaaji Cali Baxsan (Somali female singer)

Chapter III
Somali Proverbs with English Translation

In Somali oratory is never just "art of art's sake" but is bound to and part of the social life and network building. Both prose and poetry are connected with special social situations. A traditional poem has always a special message: a story to tell or an argument to advance.

Samatar, Said S. Oral poetry and Somali Nationalism: the Case of Sayyid Mohammad Abdille Hassan, 1982, p.57

・・・

Xikmaddu waa murti ka maqan aqoonta
Wisdom is content out of the knowledge 'science'

Ninkay gabadhaadu la timaadaa waa ayaankaa
He whom your daughter brings is your luck

Ummad aan dhigaal lahayni waa dhaayo aan arag lahayn
A nation with no archives is like eyes without sight 'vision'

Nin aan naynaas lahayni waa ri' gees jaban
A man who has no nickname is like a goat with a broken horn

Cadyohow ku cunay ama ku ciideeyey
Oh, you morsel, either I will chew you good or cast you aside (the selfish person takes care only by himself or herself and always his or her desire is "either my way or the high way")

Intaadan fallin ka fiirso
Look before you leap (consider all aspects of a situation before you take any action)

Hadal waa margoo kale
Speech is like a tough bite of meat 'tendon'.

Gar iyo geeriba loo siman
Death and justice affect all men equally

Hawraar murti leh iyo hilib mindi leh midna laguma margado
Neither a pithy statement nor meat eaten with a knife cause one to choke

Hawraareey ninna si kuu yiri ninna si kuu qaaday
One man's intended meaning, may be wrongly taken by another (one may convey a statement in one way and another man may understand it in another way)

Nin waliba waa hooyadii oo aan gambo lahayn
Every man is his mother without the headscarf

Haddii deg-degsiinyo door dhalaan, kaadsiinyana kiish dahab ah bay dhashaa
If haste makes hay, then patience delivers a sack of gold (when one hurries too much, one is likely to do a poor job and will have to waste time doing it over)

Rag haween ayaa kala hor mariya
It's the women who make some men succeed where others fail

Dawacadu qabatinka neefkay taqaan
A jackal is sufficiently skilled to know the vantage point from which to tackle the goat

Magooyo caano geel gelin bay ku waddaa
A mouthful 'gulp' of camel's milk is sufficient enough to sustain a camel herder half-a-day (this indicates that the nourishing quality of camel's milk, and emphasizes that a single mouthful gives a person enough energy to keep walking for half-a-day. It is also explains that a person who habitually drinks camel's milk has more physical strength and stamina than milk from other types of animals)

Cad geel seddex caana-maal baa loo socdaa

It can cause a man to travel three long days for a choice cut of camel meat

Hibo Eebbe ku siiyey habeen layskama qaado
God's grace does not come in a day's duration (don't discard your God's given grace within a night)

Shisheeye shiilo duxa ma leh
One should not expect any mercy from his enemy

Meel hal lagu qalay ma hugun la', ma hilib la', mana haad la'
A lot of meat, talk and vultures are always found around a camel's carcass (this Illustrates, that people are usually attracted to the place where a camel is slaughtered so as to partake of the meat which is enough to feed several neighboring families; hence, a lot of talk and noise is heard in such a place while the vultures are seen circling over-head)

Male rag waa mudaciyo afkood
Men's thoughts can be as sharp as the point of a needle

Haween la'aani waa hoy la'aan
Where there are no women, there is no home (no women means no shelter; therefore, as they are the main pillars of the society then without them there is no means of joyous life)

Dhubuq-dhubuq hore dhabano-hays dambay leedahay
One's carefree ways early on can result in sorrowful introspections later in life (early excesses result in later repentances, remorse and regrets; therefore, one has to behave carefully and must be balanced in his or her actions)

Rag calooshii la cayaar iyo ciil kama baxaw daran, haweenna cirkeed bogato iyo casar seexataw daran
Worst in men is he who indulges his stomach and never feels satisfied; and the worst of women is she who eats her fill and sleeps in the early afternoon (a self-indulgent man with inferiority

and a lazy gluttonous woman are both bound to have regrets later in life)

Nin rag ah haweenti ka adag, doqonna isagaa ka adag
A good man may be controlled by his wife, while lesser man dominates his

Tol waa tollane
Clanship binds (kinsmen are sewn together, because they need each other all the time and the only self-insurance they have is their unity. Therefore, they have to listen to each other and work together as closely as possible)

Hal bil qadday beri kuma dari weydo
A she-camel that went without feeding for a full month can manage to go without nourishment for one more day (a camel that stays for a month without drinking could surely stay a day more; this proverb indicates that camels are those who handle the thirst and heat more than the other animals. It also indicates how good the patient is and advises people to be very patient while awaiting the fruits of their work)

Nin aan kuu furi doonin yaanu kuu rarin
Don't let someone who will not help you to unload your camel to load it for you in the first place (means be aware the troublesome counsel of others who will not help you when you get in trouble)

Nin anni yiri dad iska sooc
Whoever says "I" has separated himself from the rest (whoever claims he is unique alienates himself from the rest of mankind)

Hadal aan fiiro loo oran iyo caano aan fiiqsi loo dhammin way kugu fogaadaan oo feerahay wax yeelaan
Both idle talk and milk consumed with haste cause an immediate distension of the rib-cage (unplanned comments or statements without caution may go too far and will hurt its originator later; so one has to be very careful and cautious with his/her words before he/she utters them)

Baahi badan, baryo badan, iyo bukaan badanba waa laysku nacaa
Both excessive neediness, too much begging and chronic ill-health can create undo resentment in others

Dhal magaalo si lagu noqdaa way dheer tahay, dhar magaalo si lagu xirtaase way dhowdahay
It is easy to don city garments, but to be truly civilized – that takes time (a person should not be judged by the clothes he or she wears; it's too easy to wear urban clothes, but too difficult to become civilized)

Geel jire geela waa wada jirtaa waana kala jirtaa
Camel herders together tend their herd but separately at the same time (it points out the fact that camel herders need to cooperate with one another in looking after their herd, which may be numerous, when they come together in a particular grazing area. At the same time, individuals have to take special care of their own animals in the combined herd)

Dagaal wiil baa ku dhinta ee wiil kuma dhasho
Conflict may result in the death of a son, not the birth of one

Hadal intuu afkaaga ku jio ayruu ammaankaaga yahay
Don't say anything that you may later regret (information is safe only while it's on your mind)

Tallo walaalki diide turaanturro ma huro
He who ignores his brother's counsel may end up stumbling

Booraan hadimo ha qodin, haddaad qodana ha dheereyn ku dhici doontidaana ma ogide
Do not dig a ditch and if you must, don't make it too deep (don't dig a deep hole of envy 'death,' as you may fall into it yourself)

Nin aad dhashay kuma dhalin

Your child is not your parent (one thinks much about his or her child as a parent, but the child doesn't understand much about his/her parent's unending love for him/her)

Majo dhooqo midba markeedaa la saaraa
If you are caught in a mud field, be sure to pull one foot at a time (pull up feet in mud one a time; whatever we do, we have to be mindfulness and patient)

Alloow aqoondarro ha nagu dillin, eexna ha nooga tegin
O' Allah don't let us die in ignorance, and don't leave us with nepotism

Wiilkaaga iyo wiilka gaalka garta u sin
Make justice equally between your son and the infidel's (unbeliever's) son

Gari Illaaheed bay taqaan
Justice knows its God only (justice is justice and it must be served justly and equally to all men)

Gari rag kama wada qosliso
Justice doesn't always make adversaries equally happy (whenever there is a verdict, one man celebrates with happiness while another man mourns with sorrow and that is the fair nature of justice)

Waano abuur baa ka horeysay
Character bests advice (a person cannot change his/her basic character once it has been formed and counseling never changes such person's behavior)

Barasho horteed ha I nicin
Get to know me, before you reject me (don't hate and stereotype something or someone before you get to know)

Durduro geel baa ku jaba

Even a camel can break a leg if it engages in careless frolicking (careless gamboling harms every one; so it's better to think twice before one does anything rash)

Rag waxaa u liita ma toshe, ma tashade iyo ma tashiishe
The worst of men is he who never sews, never consults and never economizes (there is no social value for he who can't consult his mind, can't manage his assets wisely or can't help himself otherwise)

Baydari ways bir yaqaan, bahna ways bidhaan taqaan
Hunters know each other's hunting skills, and kinsmen know each other's livestock

Dudun dugsasho iyo dareensi layskuguma daro
Don't seek shelter and fear an anthill at the same time (if you need help or advise, ask of it the one you trust the most)

Guri aan hooyo lahayni waa lama degaan
A home without a mother is like a desert (mother makes home trustworthy, happier and lovable; without her, its dark, fearful and very horrible to live in)

Quraanjo aruurtay mulac waa jiiddaa
When ants join ranks, they can even drag a lizard (unity is strength)

Gacmo wadajir bay wax ku gooyaan
When hands work together, they can achieve their objective (unity is better than division; thus, two heads are more productive than one)

Been fakatay runi ma gaarto
The truth can never catch up with a propagated lie (be proactive instead of being reactive)

Waayeel dhintay waa maktabad gubatay

The death of an elder equals the demolition of a foundation (when an elder dies he/she departs with store of experience)

Wixii tagaa tiigsimaad ma leh
What is gone is gone (a day never turns itself back again)

Fari qorrax ma qariso
A mere finger can't obscure the sun (one can not hide the truth by deception alone)

Far keliyihi fool ma dhaqdo
A finger alone cannot wash the face

Tuug tuug ma aammino
There is no honor among thieves (one dishonest person cannot trust or believe in another deceiver)

Nin aan dhul marini dhaayo maleh
He who has not traveled has no understanding (travel enhances one's experience and wisdom)

Rag aammusay iyo riyo aammusayba reerkoodii gabe
Men and goats that are silent fail their households (silent men and goats means they are sick or not doing well; so this proverb indicates that a person has to help physically and give ideas and counsel orally to his/ her family, otherwise they will be considered either sick, stupid, egotist or good-for-nothing)

Meel waa laga muuqdaa ama waa laga maqnaadaa
At your niche, either make your presence known or stay away (be active or better be absent)

Sirrow ma hodmo
A deceiver never prospers (a cheater never succeeds)

Lama huraan waa cawska jiilaal
Necessity is like the withered leaves of winter (they may be unpalatable but one must avail himself of them)

Seddex lalama dego: kaa doonay kaa diiday; kugu dire kaa dige; iyo kaa daare kaa danqaabe
Don't pitch your tent next to either of the following three: the ungrateful, the instigator, or the gossip-monger (he who always needs your help but is naughty; he who always advises you to stir up a conflict but snitches on you, or the gossip-monger)

Dhaxal goroyo dhebed baa leh
The partridge often inherits the ostrich's nest (people inherit each other's wealth in accordance to how closely related they are)

Farriini waa qaan
Trust is like indemnity (the messenger is honor-bound to convey his message to the designated person)

Fartaada xumi filiq-filiq kaagama harto
Your bad finger may not be easily shaken off (a weak link such as one's injured small finger cannot be easily disposed of; thus, one's bad relatives, friends or countrymen are weak links that will not go away; so it is essential to handle these problems with much care)

Labo waa ku hor socotaa: hawo iyo hunguri; labana waa ku hareer socotaa: faa'iido iyo khasaaro; labana waa ku daba socotaa: gabow iyo geeri
There are three life-long companions: two walk before you, desire and ambition; two walk alongside you, fortune and misfortune; and two walk behind you, old age and death (good and bad things tend to happen in groups)

Labo waa la dheefshaa "indhaha," labana waa la dhawraa "gacmaha," labana waa la dhibaa "lugaha."
Two needs that must be nourished: "eyes," two needs to be cared for: "hands" and two needs that must be fatigued: "legs."

Samo lama wada laysan karo
It is always time to do good

War la helaa talo la helaa
Information facilitates decision-making (information triggers decision)

Samataliye sedkii waa janno
To advise good is true faith

Labo waa la dheefshaa "indhaha," labana waa la dhawraa "gacmaha," labana waa la dhibaa "lugaha."
Two needs that must be nourished: "eyes," two needs to be cared for: "hands" and two needs that must be fatigued: "legs."

Hal xaraan ahi nirig xalaal ah ma dhasho
A stolen she-camel begets no holy calf (indicates that a stolen or any other properties that you attain illegally will never make you happy and its income or profit is illegal too, simply because it's not yours)

Halmaan hadal kuma jiro
Forgetfulness is not part of speech (inadvertent mistake in speech is not good enough to be counted)

Indho jacayl isma eegaan
Eyes in love do not dare stare at each other (lovers' eyes are bashful)

Nin weyn wadkii waa yaqaan
An old man is mindful of his impending death (means a wise person knows what's good or bad for him/her)

Aabbahay baa geel lahaan jiray, anigaa dameer leh baa dhaanta
To claim I have a donkey bests the claim "my dad had camels"

Nin dhintay kabihiisaa dhaama
A dead man's shoes are worth more to the living than he

Saxan saxan ku gud, saanna saan ku gud

Cover a plate with a plate and a step with a step (a favor should be repaid with another favor)

Labaatan jir geedkaad ku beerato lixdan jir ayaad ku goosataa
At age sixty you reap the fruit of the tree that you have sown at age twenty (the amount of effort you put into something while young and energetic determines how much you will get out of it at a later age)

Miro gunti ku jira miro geed saaran looma daadsho
Never discard fruits in your pocket for fruits in some tree (something you already have is better than something you might later get)

Ooyi doonow ayaar joog
He who will cry first 'in a fight or debate' ought to stay back (one has to stay out of trouble if he/she can't handle the situation later on)

Haani guntay ka tolantaa
A water vessel is sewn from the bottom up (everything starts from the base foundation not from the top)

Hadal badan dan baa dhaanta
Action speaks louder than words (too much talk without benefit is a waste of time, while even a little action goes a long way)

Meel il laga la'yahay haddii aad tagto il baa lays tiraa
If you go to a place inhabited by one-eyed people, poke out one of your own (when traveling, always observe the customs of the local people)

Gacmo wadajir bay wax ku gooyaan
Hands achieve more when they work in unison (unity can solve a problem much better, easier and even quicker than disunity)

Waari mayside war ha kaa haro

Since you will not live forever better leave a good name behind (keep your reputation good while still alive so you will not leave a bad legacy behind after your death)

Wan weyn indhihiisu cirka ma arkaan ilaa la gawraco
An old ram's eyes never see the sky until it's slaughtered

War la qabo xiiso maleh
Old news is boring (to repeat news that has been exposed earlier is uninteresting)

Waraf meel dhow buu ku dhacaa warna meel dheer buu ku dhacaa
A sling shot may fall short, but news travels far

Wixii qof dhibbaa tol ma dhibo
What troubles one person need not trouble to whole family

Xaqu feeruhuu ka dillaacaa
Injustice is ultimately exposed (injustice ruptures the ribs)

Xoolo rag farana ka tirsan feerana ka xisaaban
Men's wealth is countable by hand and remembered by heart

Yeelaa waa illoobaa la yeelaase ma illoobo
He who injuries may easily forget but the injured never forget

Runi rag kama nixiso
The truth does not make men squirm

Doqoni halkii lagu dagaalay ogeyde, halka lagu heshiiyey ma ogayn
The fool always remembers the scene of hostilities, but not the site of reconciliation

Hubsiimo hal baa la siistaa
Certitude is worth a she-camel (camels are the mainstay of the Somali economy, so this proverb is pointing out that to make sure of something, even if you have to give your beloved she-camel or

whatever will make possible for you to know the reality of something instead of straying or lying)

Beeni raad ma leh
A lie does not leave footprints (if a liar tries to defend or prove his/her lie as truth, he/she will never find a way to verify it)

Maroodigu takarta saaran ma arkee kan kale takarta saaran buu arkaa
An elephant doesn't see the gadfly on its back but can easily see the gadfly on another elephant's back (people see each other's negativities; but it's much harder for some one to see his/her own faults)

Biyo kaa badan iyo dad kaa badaniba way ku harqiyaan
Both a torrent of water and a crowd of your enemies are liable to drown you (it's not wise for one to face an out-numbering hostile people or any natural force that might overwhelm him/her)

Nin tuur lihi siduu u seexdo isagaa og
A humpback best knows how he sleeps (every one best knows how to solve his/her own problems)

Mar I dage Alle ha dago mar labaad I dagase anays dagay
He who deceives me once, may Allah deceive him, but if the same man deceives me again, I deserve to be deceived

Ninkaad barashadiisa rabto, jid la mar, jidiin la cun ama jabad la deg
If you wish to learn someone's true nature; go on a journey with him/her, share a meal with him/her or become to his/her next-door neighbor

Nin kuu digey kuma dilin
He who warns in advance is not likely to kill you (The man who fore-warns you is like the one who saves your life; someone who gives you a verbal warning before starting any hostilities with you cannot be blamed for harming you afterwards. if one admonishes

you before he/she does harm to you, is the one who must be listened with care and left alone in peace; otherwise you will share the blame with him/her if anything untoward happens)

Dantiisa mooge, maro duug ah horteed buu dhammaadaa
One who ever neglects his/her affairs wears out quicker than an old rag

Gar diid waa Alle diid
The man who refuses to heed sound counsel is like a man who rejects his own God (a person who disobeys the civil laws of his society is like someone who denies God's existence)

Wax nin la toosani nin la tuur leh
One man's gravy is another man's poison (what appears like the right path to one man may look like the wrong course to another)

Doqon hana gargaarsan, hana u gargaarin
Don't help the fool and don't ask him/her for help (stay away dealing with fools)

Nin waliba ceesaantii ceel keen
Every man comes to the well with his "young" she-goat (everyone can only be proud of whatever he/she possesses)

Gees lo'aad kulaylkaa lagu gooyaa
Shape the cow's horn while it's still hot (act at the best possible time); this is the equivalent of the English saying, *"strike the anvil while the iron is hot"*

Dani waa seeto
Need binds like a tether (if someone's need is very critical for a solution then he/she has to face the reality and try to find an absolute answer)

Dantaada masale ey ayaa loogu seexdaa
Sleep for your interest even on a mat made out of a dog's hide (you have to try everything possible to satisfy your critical

interest; therefore, you have to keep your self-interest as close to you as the mat you sleep on)

Dhurwaaga qaysha iyo kan aammusan keebaa darran?
Which is more dangerous, a hyena that howls or a silent one? (It's easier for one to defend his/her self from the openly threatening person than the silent and unpredictable hypocrite one)

Dhagax taabasho iyo tuujin waa iskugu mid
A stone is a stone whether you touch it or squeeze (if someone tries to convince something a logger-head, the final result will be the same as it was before)

Rubad go'day iyo roob galbeed midna sooma noqdaan
Neither a dead being nor a rain that heads in a westerly direction ever returns (it's a Somali belief that the rain never comes from the west)

Nin is-faanshay waa ri' is-nuugtay
He who praises himself is like a she-goat that suckles itself (if you deserve any praise it must come from the society that you live with otherwise your boasting will deminish your dignity)

Geel la'aani waa caano la'aan, caano la'aanna waa nolol la'aan
Where there are no camels there are no milk, and where there are no milk there is no life (the absence of camels is like the absence of milk and the absence of milk are like the absence of life)

Nin isfaanshay fallar baa maqan
He who praises himself is lacking somehow (boasting is a taboo in Somali culture, so this proverb is indicating that he/she who always brags is like a one who is feeling some inferiority; therefore one may think boasting as the only useful weapon to elevate his/her social position)

Hadal badan haamo lagama buuxsho
Too much talk does not fill vessels (talkativeness with no reasoning is always useless)

Shabeel aadan dilin haraggii lama beeciyo
Kill the tiger before you sell his skin

Beentaada hore runtaada dambay u daran tahay[195]
Your earlier lies undermine your later truths (if someone is accustomed to lying then one day his/her lie will get him/her in trouble)

Sac geeso weyn ma hargalo lagamana hargalo
A bull with long horns never rests and would not allow others to rest

Nin xeel badani ma xirmo
A clever man never finds himself at wit's end (a trickery man is never caught; experienced being always gets a solution to his/her problems easily)

Gurbaan garabka ha kuugu jiro ama gacalkaa ha kuu hayo
A drum must be in your possesssion or your best friend has to hold it for you (always hold your drum 'weapon' by your side or in the custody of your close relatives or friend indeed)

Habaar ma dhaafo tiro ariya lahow oo tolkaa taajir u ahow
There is no worse curse than owning one-hundred goats (instead of camels) and being considered the richest of your clan

Geel rag iyo Rabbaa dhaqa
Camels are guarded either by men or God (camels need men and God to safeguard them, and they always need the services of strong men to safeguard their security. The camel-owner also needs God's blessing in maintaining these valued animals. This proverb is pointing out that every vital and important thing, such as the camels, and one's nation needs very strong, charismatic, visionary and honorable sons and daughters to defend with the help and blessings of God)

---

[195] Remember Cali Beenaale (Ali the lair) early childhood Somali folktale!

Shir looma wada uunsiyo
All truth is not always to be told

Dhagar qabe dhulkaa u dhaqdhaqaaqa
A guilty conscience needs no accuser

Haan qarroorkeed reer tolkaa looguma taliyo
Never counsel your kinsmen on vessel's residue liquid (you cannot be a leader of your kinsmen when all you can offer is the last drops at the bottom of a milk-vessel)

Haddaad dhimanayso dhareerka waa layska duwaa
Even if you're on your death-bed, don't let your drool run (always be dignified with the highest virtue of yourself)

Haddaan la kala roonaan roob ma da'o
It may not rain when some don't act more responsibly than the rest (when two people or more are dealing together every one has to keep the calmness and patient has to be observed all the time, otherwise nothing will go easy and a positive result will be out of the question)

Kab xume ma haree kab laawaa hara
A badly shod man is more likely to win a foot-race than one without any shoes (It is the shoeless man that falls behind not the bad-shod; therefore, one who has something in hand is always better off than he who has nothing)

Kor waayeel waa wada indho
A wise old man sees all (an elderly and experienced person has an abundance of wisdom; thus, his/her far-sightedness is always in his/her treasury)

Kuugu dhiijiyaa loogu dhiijiyaa
You milk a beast for they who milk for you (generosity works both ways, so you must be generous to your helpers when they are in need)

Abaal soo deg-dega rag iyo geel baa leh, mid raagana haween iyo lo' baa leh
Generousity belongs to men and camels, niggardliness belongs to women and cattle (men and camels are quick with gratitude, while women and cattle are most slow with it as it says primitively)

Darandooriyaaba naas-naasi
Whoever milks abundantly could suffer later (whoever acts hastily may encounter later disappointment; nothing is granted in this life so one has to be aware of whatever change comes and has to face it bravely)

Hunnu-hunnu hadal ma'ahan, himbiriirsina wax arag ma'ahan
Talking gibberish is no speech, and squinting is no sight (means one has to clarify or prove his/her point to be properly understood)

Ruuxii isha daba Aadmigaa arka, kii uurka dabana Allaa arka
People can see those who squint, but only God can see those who harbor ill-will in their hearts

Ragow barasho geeloow rarasho
Men, you have to get to know them; camels, you know them by the load they can carry (you will know someone well when you meet with him/her and you may evaluate him/her afterwards, and you will know and respect your he-camel when you know his strength and capability)

Belaayo ama guur bay ku tiraahdaa ama guurso
The messengers of evil may tell you to move away "migrate" or marry (one has to be well-prepared when he/she wants to marry or move or do other things; because one needs a lot of preparation and strength, physically, economically, morally and emotionally; hence, you must plan well for your actions in advance)

Dheri la kor taagan yahay ma karo
A watched pot never boils

Raqba waa ku raggeed
Every problem must be solved by its own local people (every problem, legal matter or case must be solved by its present or original people)

Harag libaax haadi ma jiiddo
Even a lion's hide is enough to scare the vultures away (no one will dare to harm or hit a strong and brave person, even after he/she dies)

Cimri tegey ceeb laguma sagootiyo
One should not end one's old age with a shameful act (when someone is old enough or becomes an elder it's important that that person behave to the best of his/her ability and become a good model to others and also to keep away himself/herself from shameful things not to dishonour or disgrace themselves)

Doqoni cad carro loogu tuuray calaf ma moodo
Fools don't take a morsel of food thrown in the sand for their sustenance (only a fool refuses a morsel of food because it has been cast in the dust; never ever disregard a positive offer even if its not completely satisfying your need!)

Ninkaan wiilkiisa geel u tabcini, geeridiisuu sugaa
He who leaves no camels for his son foresees his own death (It is said that, "camels bestow great honor and prestige to the owner." Therefore, a man who leaves no camels for his children when he passes away is considered to have lived in vain and that his offspring would have no secure future)

Haddaad doonayso in aad malab gurato, ha dilaacin xabag-barsheedka
If you want to collect honey, don't break the honeycomb (one has to be very careful whatever he/she wants to achieve safely and not to spoil the result)

Hadal ha yaraado danna ha ahaado

Make speech short and aim high (one has to manage his/her way of speech and has to talk about the importance of his/her intention effectively and objectively)

Haddii lagu sheelo waa lays sheegaa, haddii lagu sheegana waa lays sheelaa
If you are ignored, speak for yourself but if you are introduced, remain quite and polite

Abeeso far loo taagay fanaxay u booddaa
If you point a finger at an adder, it will jump at the chance (this proverb is about the greedy person who has never known 'enough' but always tries to take everything from others whether it's friend or foe)

Gafuur cawo ninkii buuruu dhibaa
He who pouts in the dark only punishes his lips (haughtiness in the night harms he who has a grudge; making your feelings unknown will hurt you and only you, but when you show it or tell to your partner healing is possible)

Atoor sagaaro intiisa waa ku duq
A male dikdik will always appear old (it's difficult to tell the dikdik's age whether it's young or old; so this proverb is a euphemism for the younger person who is more wise and responsible than his/her age with an articulating behavior)

Shimbirba shimbirkiisuu la duulaa
Birds of same feather flock together (people tend to associate with their own kind, professional or any other affiliations that apply)

Biyo sacabadaadaa looga dhergaa
You can drink enough water from the palms of your hands (it's only you who can choose the way to success, no one else can help you if you are not ready to help yourself)

Calool-adayg waa Illaahay wehelkii

Courage is God's companion (courage, bravery, patience and boldness are all God's gifts and one can overcome all his/her hardships and will be a good example to others if he/she shows these good characteristics)

Daacadi ma hungowdo
Honesty never meets with disappointment (frankness, sincerity and faithfulness lead people to success and its bearer never goes with empty-handedness)

Dab aan kulaylkiisa la arag dambaskiisa lagama leexdo
No one steps aside from ashes whose ambers' heat has not been felt (the inexperienced is more likely to mistakenly fall into the traps of calamity)

Dab munaafaq shiday miskiin baa ku gubta
When a hypocrite ignites a fire only the innocent burn

Doc ka yeer daankaa lagu dhuftaa
Break the double-talker's jaw in order to silence him (try to control firmly the one who doesn't wait his/her own turn to talk)

Gadaal ka gaar waa goob dumis
The late-comer can only cause chaos (when one comes late, has to patiently wait to understand the whole basis and concepts of the affair '*shir*' before he takes his/her turn, otherwise his/her blind interference will disturb the procedure)

Iimaan Allaa uur buuxsha
Only faith in Allah can fill one's heart (confidence, faith, belief and contentment are what make people happy and not greedy; this proverb points out that the greedy are never satisfied with anything but are always hungry and thirsty and eager to fulfill their unrealistic dreams)

Nin yari intuu laan ka boodo ayuu talana ka boodaa
A young man may jump over advice as much as he jumps over the branches of a high-tree (this shows how an inexperienced lad

could miss advise, counsel, decision, opinion or proposal; so always he/she needs the elders' wits and wisdoms)

Eray xumi urug kici
A bad word can stir up deep-seated emotions (an abusive word can breed ill-will and may create, raise, agitate or renew memories of emotional pain, grief, worry and depression; therefore it's not good for someone to talk about it and farther harm the victim)

Adduunyo waa sheeko iyo shaahid
Knowledge is obtained by either through hearsay or by direct experience

Ninkii seexdaa sicii dibi dhalaa
He who sleeps may later find out that his cow had delivered a male calf, instead of the preferred female calf (if you're expecting "want" a good outcome you have to work for it)

Laba kala bariday kala warla'
Two who have stayed separately in distances may have no knowledge of each other's fortunes (or misfortunes)

Nin aan naynaas lahayni waa ri' gees jaban
A man with no nickname is like a goat with a broken horn (nicknames are very useful and abundant in Somali culture, therefore this proverb indicates that a man with no nickname has no social recognition because most of the time nicknames are more popular than one's given name; but the same is not true for women)

Ood kaa fogi kuma dhaxan tirto
A distant thicket can't provide you with protection from cold drafts (a distant fortune never satisfies one's needs)

Nin aan war sugini waran ma sugo
He who can't wait for a word will not wait for a spear (one who has no patience to wait and listen to the news will not have the

brave heart to wait for a spearshot during combat; this points out one of the coward person's characteristics)

Nin gar daran ma guuleysto
He who mistreats others will ultimately fail (one who starts the wrong offense and attacks will never succeed because provocation is the only weapon of cowards and Allah helps not provocateurs)

Nin hooyadii qorrax u jiiday sodohdii ma hariyo
He who exposes his own mother to the heat of the sun will not likely bring his mother-in-law into the shade (parents are very important to every society and this saying indicates that the one who wrongs his/her parents will not be kind and good to others)

Nin hadal badshey ma dhammeyn, nin yareeyeyna ma hambayn
He who talks a lot may not have said everything and he who talks less may not leave anything out (this indicates that one's talk has to be as short as possible and to the point)

Nin qayrkii loo xiirayoow soo qoyso adiguna
When they execute your kin, you may expect to be next (whatever affects your equal can affect you too, so you have to learn from his/her misfortune and must prepare yourself with an appropriate precaution)

Madax muuqda iyo mindi saawir ah midna lagama quusto
One may still have expectations of some loser nearby or a dull knife close at hand (desire never ends)

Markay ceelalyo heshiiso ayaa xooluhu biyo cabbaan
Livestock drinks water comfortably when its owners are at peace (every problem is solvable if people understand each other and follow an orderly process)

Nin aan kibir jebin maroodi ma jebsho
An elephant does not hobble whose arrogance doesn't hobble him (modesty, humility and simplicity are more important than arrogance for everyone)

Dhubuq-dhubuq hore dhabana hays dambay leedahay
Marry in haste, repent at leisure

Canaan la'aan carruuri ma korto
Spare the rod spoils the child

Nin habaarani ma har galo
Cursed man never finds peace and repose (someone cursed by his parents or the people he harmed is always distrustful, with a guilty conscience)

Aqool xumo abaar ka darran
Mismanagement is worse than drought (good management is the first sign of happiness and success, therefore it's always important and indispensable; otherwise one who is accustomed to mismanagement will remain in pain and hopelessness)

Qosol badani qoonsimaad buu dhalaa
Much laughter arouses the listener's suspicions

Nin qoyani biyo iskama dhawro
A wet man need not avoid water

Af qoyani hadal ma daayo
A living mouth does not give up talk

Ayax teg eelna reeb
When locust leaves, it always leaves misery behind

Nin soori qaaday nin seefi qaaday baa dhaama
A man killed by a sword is preferable to one given to greediness

Doqoni laba iyo toban indhood bay leedahayoo, midna shisheeyahay ku aragtaa, kow iyo tobanka kalana sokeeyahay ku aragtaa
The fool has twelve eyes, one guards against her enemy, and other eleven guard against own kin

Ninkii soo joog laga waayo soo jiifsaa laga helaa
The reckless ultimately learn the importance of caution (one who refuses to stay in peace and always wrongs others ends up with calamity)

Af jooga looma adeego
You shouldn't speak for one who is present

Qori iyo qiiqiisaba waa laysla tuuraa
Throw the fire-stick away along with its smoke (always leave the unimportant things behind and go forward to do something usable)

Inta dhogortaadu dhaqantahaa la dhawrsadaa
Take care while your virtue is still intact (always behave with caution and save your reputation and dignity carefully)

Arrad waa dan, uskagse waa doqoniimo
Lack of proper clothing is acceptable, but living with dirt is foolishness (one has to be always as hygienic as possible)

Meel waa laga muuqdaa ama waa laga maqnaadaa
Be counted or you better stay away (one has to be active and helpful when needed by his/her society or it is best if they don't make their presence known)

Hansi gabdheed iyo habaar waalid midna kaama haro
Neither a young woman's evil eye nor a parent's curse can be outlived

Ratiga dambe ratiga hore saanqaadkiisuu leeyahay
The lead camel sets the course (everyone behaves the same way that his/her parents or mentors behave)

Run iyo ilkaba waa la caddeeyaa
Make both teeth and truth abundantly clear (one has to tell the truth straightforward and try to prove his/her point clearly to distinguish it from bogus claims)

Caqli fiyoobi jir fiyow buu leeyahay
A sound in mind in a sound body

Samraa sedkii waa helaa
He who remains patient finds his daily ration (patience is good; thus, this proverb tells us that he/she who shows patience and calmness is the one who gets his/her allotment and provisions most likely)

Ari jir ma kala abaal weydo
Herders tend to assist each other (people in same profession are always in need of each other and everyone brings his/her problems to his/her collueges)

Shimbirtii duulduul badani af libaax bay ku dhacdaa
A bird that flies about carelessly may end up in the jaws of a lion (he/she who is accustomed to doing things or saying words always without care finally may face an unprecedented problem and pay an unnecessary price for his/her mistake; so one has to be very careful with his/her actions before they bring calamity upon him/her)

Sida laysku xigo layskuma cunee sida layskugu calaf leeyahay baa laysku cunaa
One eats not necessarily his own kin's provisions, but eats whatever is written for him by God (everyone's allotments were written by Almighty God, so he/she eats of it and it's not wise to hate or insult your relative that he/she is feeding others while you're not fed by him/her)

Sirmaqabe saabbaa biyo u cesha
The faithful are saved even by drift-wood (an honest person never astrays out or loses his grip; therefore to be honest is to be blessed)

Abeeso yaanay dhul u ekaan kugu dilin, wadaadna yaanu dad u ekaan kugu dilin
Don't let an adder deceive you by hiding in the sand or a bush-priest by appearing like a normal human being (always make sure

to double check what you're doing and whom you're associating with and don't stereotype someone before you know him/her well)

Albaab furan lama galee, weji furan baa la galaa
It's not an open door but an open heart one should be received with (if you open your door to someone but you didn't treat them with respect, that hospitality is nothing and it's a wasted effort and energy; so, it's better to show your heart-felt generosity instead of offering an empty hearted hospitality to someone)

Hawo iyo hoos galbeed midna lama gaaro
Both desire and evening shades are unreachable (human desire never ends, therefore one has not to obsess to fulfill all his/her dreams in one day, but has to live according to the reality on the ground)

Taladaan la ruugin waa lagu rafaadaa
Unexamined counsel can bring unbearable consequences (counsel decided without observations and second thoughts is harmful; therefore everything that one is doing must be examined and decided carefully before rushing to judgment)

Tuf 'godob' qabaa takareysan
A guilty man may be exposed by his nervous fidgeting (he who resented is he who is quarantined. If one owes for damages that he caused to another, till he/she is cleared, he/she will feel guilty about it and will never be at peace)

Hadal lama wadaagee caanaa la wadaagaa
People should not talk all at once but they may pass a bowl of milk around to share (this proverb is pointing out that when one is talking the other has to wait his/her turn, because there is no understanding when everybody talks all at once)

Waayeel iyo ummulisaba siday wax u ogyihiin uma sheegaan
An elderly person and a mid-wife do not reveal all that they had experienced (this proverb is about the morality and the

confidentiality of one's profession; and advises one has to keep the secrets dearly without shaming, disclosing or smearing the concerned ones)

Walaaloow waxaan lagu helin waran laguma helo
What you can't achieve by asking nicely may not be achieved by the tip of the spear (peace is better and more beneficial than war, so this proverb advises that one has to use diplomacy with decency before he/she decides to fight)

Haddii malag dhawaaqaayo miidaamo dhego male
When the angel of death is on his way the prospective victim may not always hear his approach (if something from the Almighty is to happen no one else can delay it and it will happen as ordered)

Xarig habeen iyo xaal sokeeyaba ninkii ogaa baa fura
Only he who ties a knot in the dark or has secret knowledge of the affairs of a kinsman can solve such mysteries

Hadal iyo hilbaba waa la saafaa
Both talk and meat should be best sliced thin

Nin maalin ma gaartid "ninka kaa faras dheereeya;" ninna sannad ma gaartid "ninka xoolihiisu daaqa kaaga horeeyeen;" ninna weligaa ma gaartid "ninka kaa naagta fiican."
You catch up not a man for a day and that is the man whose horse is faster than yours; and you catch up not a man for a year and that is the man whose livestock reached the virgin grazing grounds before yours; and you catch up not a man forever and that is the man who has a better spouse than yours. (This proverb is very important and meaningful and it indicates the importance of women, their usefulness and how they differentiate the men of same quality at birth later in their life time; and it's absolutely true that women are the ones who create the bonds between men)

Baadiyi nin aan lahayn bay ag joogtaa
Stray stock is always in the vicinity of some one who doesn't own it

Cadar ceel kaama furto
The morning cloud never lasts for the day

Barti yaqaan bari uma kororto
The man who only knows his particular advantage is unlikely to prosper in the long run

Rag gogoshi waa nabad, geel xeradi waa rag, yaabis iidaankiina waa gaajo
Men are best served by peace, camel's corrals are best guarded by men, and food without seasoning is the harbinger of hunger

Libaax nin ganayna og nin galladayna og
A lion can easily differentiate between he who intends to harm him and who means him well

Baqashii fardo la mirataa ka mid bay is mooddaa
A mule that grazes with horses comes to think of itself as a horse

Nin weyn oo qawl ka dhacay waa geed qolofi ka dhacday
An elder's broken promise is like a leaf that falls from its tree

Lax walba shillalkay is dhigtaa lagu gawracaa
Every ewe is slaughtered by the place of its own choice

Nin aan kuu furi doonin yaanu kuu xirin (rarin)
Don't let that he who will not untie a knot for you tie it for you in the first place

Nin naagi waddo iyo rati rati wado midna kaama leexdaan
A man guided by a woman and a stud-camel led by another are unlikely to get out of your way

Nin gu' kaa weyni il gumuxeedna kaa weyn
He who is older than you by a season is more knowledgeable than you by at least once glance

Qun yar socde qodaxi ma muddo

A thorn does not prick he who steps cautiously

Cayaar la'aan caqligu wuu caabuqaa
All work and no play make the mind a dull heart

Tiisa kalkaalaa tu kalana ku dara
He who helps himself can help others as well

Ceel aadan ka biyo gaarayn lama qodo
Kindle not the fire that you can't put out

Xaglo laaban xoolo kuma yimaadaan
Where there is no effort there is no gain

Habba kuu darraadee dad waa ina adeerkaa
One still needs people even if they are not of much help (although they are not good for you, but still all men are your cousins)

Fuley far looma godo
Don't show your pended finger to a coward (cowards never take risks, so if you point your finger at something, he will think that you're showing him an enemy; thus, don't expect a coward to stand by you!)

Nin daad qaaday xunbo cuskay
A drowning man clutches all straws (when one is hopeless he/she thinks that everything can safe him/her, so it's normal for one to try every possible way in order to survive)

Waxay ishu raacdo yaa uurkuna jeclaadaa
Whatever pleases the eye the heart desires (whatever pleases the eye is what the heart craves)

Libaax nin aan aqoon baa lax ka rita
Someone who doesn't know the true nature of a lion may chase him to recover a stolen ewe (it's easy for an inexperienced man to take all kinds of risks without considering the consequences)

Caado la gooyaa caro Allay leedahay
Customs rule the law

Nin weyn tag lama yiraahdo ee wuxuu ku tagaa la tusaa
Don't tell an elder to leave, but show him a reason for him to leave (it's impolite for one to dictate to an elder and tell him what to do, but it's more acceptable and proper to persuade him gently with diplomacy)

Bidaari sibiq bay kugu gashaa
Baldness often starts abruptly (everything that you are not aware of comes suddenly, so it's necessary for one to be very careful by his/herself and to be cautious all the time in order to be safe and sound)

Nin walba qumanihiisaa qoorta ugu jira
Every man considers himself correct (every person thinks that he/she is the most perfect person in his/her own society)

Haddaad nabad doonayso adiga ha lagaa helo
If you want peace, it must first come from you (be nice and respectful to others if you want respect from them)

Qoori xero kuma heshiiso
Studs in a single enclosure are bound to fight with one another (two braves of equal strength are unlikely to coexist peacefully in the same space, so one has to lead and the other has to follow)

Laba qaawani isma qaaddo
Two who are destitute can't help each other

Nin kaad kabo ka tolanayso, kabihiisaa la eegaa
Before you ask a cobbler to fashion a pair of shoes for you, first take a good look at his own shoes

Xaniinyo laysma dhibaadsho
Bravery is not given as a gift (no one can give someone else the natural abilities that one was born with such as bravery, sincerity,

good health, strength, etc., so one must not expect such virtues from someone else)

Qof wax ku siiyaa badan, qof kula taliyaase yar
There are many people who will give you things, but few who can give you good advise (counsel is so more important than any other thing, so he who helps you with sound advise is more helpful than others who give you material things and one has to take and keep that advise dearly)

Bello intay kaa maqan tahay, qayrkaa bay ku maqan tahay
While calamity (evil) is away from you, it's probably after your kin (if one is living well without trouble and hardship, he then has to know that everybody is not necessarily having that sort of luck; he has to know that more people are living in misery; so he has to behave and has to work hard and not to face that same calamity in turn)

Bello dhego la qabtay leedahaye dabo la qabto me leh
Calamity (evil) has ears to catch but not a tail to hold onto (one has to prepare his or herself before any problems occur; and has to know if that hardship is not prepared for before hand it will be too late to cope with when it finally comes)

Salaad waliba siday kuu qabataa loo tukadaa
One prays every prayer at its right time

Sir naagood lagama sal gaaro
Women's deception has no bottom (women are more conniving than men as this proverb indicates, so one has to ask them to solve the problems they have created)

Sidee xeego loo xagtaa ilkana u nabad galaan?
How does one gnaw the bark of a palm tree's sweet seeds and save one's teeth at the same time? (This proverb is indicating that one has to solve a problem without losing anything; so one has to use skill, patience and wisdom)

Haweeni waa tii eraygaaga maqasha, hantidaadana xafidda
A good woman is the one who listens 'obeys' to what you have to say and safeguards your property

Geesi kol buu dhintaa, fuleyna kun jeer
Coward dies many times before his death, but brave dies once

Rag waa haween hambadood
Men are what women have left behind

Nin geed geli jiray, geed looma galo!
Don't expect to ambush an expert ambusher! (Don't try to cheat someone with the same trick that he already knows)

Geel laba jir soo wada mar
All camels live through the age of two (everyone can understand what he /she has already acquired)

Gaal dil gartiisana sii
Slay the unbeliever but don't deny him his rights (as we said before, "justice is equal to all men," therefore everyone deserves his/her piece of justice without discrimination on the basis of creed, color, religion, ethnicity or national origin)

Hal booli ahi nirig xalaal ah ma dhasho
A looted she-camel bears no honest calf (illegal property never makes one happy and wealthy because one day its rightful owner will discover and claim it)

Habar fadhidaa legden la fudud yahay
A seated old woman may think wrestling is an easy sport (naïve people think everything is either too easy or too difficult-- and nothing between)

Nin fadhiga kuugu jeeda looma sare kaco
Don't get up to show yourself for someone who sees you sitting (if one can't help you from his/her kindness and generosity when

they know that you are in need, then better stay away and don't ask them for help)

Been beelo kuma negaadaan
A lie never puts campers at ease

Geel fudaydna kuma rimo fudaydna kuma dhalo
No gain without pain

Reer waa naag
Any household that prospers must have a woman behind it (this acknowledges the crucial importance of woman's role in society)

Naag la'aan waa naf la'aan
To be without a woman is to be without life (this indicates the crucial importance of a woman's support)

Kal caano galeen kas ma galo
Reason and a chest that has produced milk do not go together

Harag sagaaro iiga kac mooyaane iiga durug ma leh
A dikdik's hide has only enough space to accommodate one person

Farta iyo halka bugtaa iyagaa is og
Fingers best know an ailing part in one's body (everybody knows well what troubles him than anyone else)

Seddex ka dheerow: dhiig sokeeye, xaaraan iyo basari guurkeed
Avoid three things in life at all cost: shedding kinsmen's blood; engaging in religiously prohibited acts; or marrying a slovenly woman (this applies to both genders; if there are slovenly women, yes, there are slovenly men too)

Geeduhu siday isku xigaan bay isku xoqaan
Trees scrape each other as they adjoin (relatives and friends work closer)

Habar dheregtay, dhasheed ma oga
A woman who has her fill does not know her children

Haweeen seddex ma jecla: ma hambeeye, ma dhalle; iyo fakhri liita
Women dislike three kinds of husbands: those who leave no food on the platters atfter a meal; those who are impotent; and those who are hopelessly poor

Cilmi dumar ninkii diida waa u carruur la'aan
The man who rejects a woman's knowledge will surely be without issue (women know better about children's ailments than men, so men have to accept that truth if they want their children to live)

Habar walba habeenkeed
Every woman has her 'lucky or unlucky' night (suggests that a mother needs luck to raise good and responsible children, many women take the moral education of their children firmly in hand)

Naag waliba waa ninkeeda
Every woman belongs to the kin group of her husband

Doqon baa dabadeeda Illaahay ku liibaanaa
God gave the useless wife victory through her hind-sight (a slovenly wife who gives birth to sons would be emotionally and economically secure)

Hadal nin badiyeyna ma dhameyn, nin yareeyeyna ma hambayn
The talkative man never reaches the end of speech and the quiet man never leaves a left-over

Xoolahaagu xero ha kuugu jiraan ama xeer ha kaaga maqnaadaan
Keep your wealth close at hand or give it away as a gift

Naari meel qabow ma leh
There are no cool corners in Hell

Guul lagaaga dambeeyaa guul ma ahan

A victory is no victory if you are not the ultimate winner

Rag waxaan ilmaha iga soo qabta ahayn waa la kulmaa
Men may encounter every adversity short of delivering a baby

Guri fiican lama gato ee jaar fiican baa la gataa
Choose your neighbor before you choose your home

Af-garooc afkiisaa meel xun dhiga
An inarticulate man's words may land him in disaster (because his words would not be adequate enough to defend himself or prove his point clearly)

Xeer waa xeer xarragana waa lagama tagaan
An obligation is an obligation, but one should not lose his dignity over it (a law is a law but nobility is indispensable; means if you win your case in court, still you have to respect the opposite side)

Tol xeer lihi cayr ma'ahan
Those who have strong kinship ties and regulations should never fear destitution (kinsmen with a strong customary law are not poor)

Guney xeerkaa labooy xaalka
Law by its justice and two by their agreed customs (every law preserves it's justly justice and every two who has their differences either uses by that general law or their own norms if there has been any of its kind that they agreed upon)

Oodi ab ka dhow
Nearest is dearest (neighborhood ties are stronger than lineage ties (neighborhoodness is more important than maternal/faternal blood relationship)

Nin kaa af-badani dhaxalka aabbahaana waa ku seejiyaa
A man who is more eloquent than you can even rob you of your inheritance

Askari xanaaqay waa ciir faadhay

An angry cop is like fermenting milk

Talo qofkeedaa ku nool ee iyadu kuma noola
Good counsel serves its owner, but the owner does not serve his/her counsel

Talo xumo tog baas bay kaa riddaa
Bad counsel may cause you to fall into an abyss

Talo walaalki diide turaanturro ma huro
He who ignores his brother's good counsel meets a bitter end (loggerheadness is an altimate defeat)

Nin is waalaba waabiyaa hela
The aggressive man ultimately encounters a more aggressive man

Af qoslay ilko kuma qarsoomaan
There are no hidden teeth in a laughing mouth

Madax meel ka sareeya oo la salaaxaa ma jirto
There is no higher point in the body than the top of the head to caress (if one becomes a leader for his people, he has to lead his followers to the best of his abilities while his decisions will impact every thing under his leadership)

Nin cir weyni calooshiisa waa la col
A gluttonous man is at war with his own stomach (because if there is no enough food to fill his belly then he will be always angry and hungry)

Baryadaada baahidaadaa lala sugtaa
Don't beg until you are desperate (it's best to perservere before one resorts to begging)

Dawaco halkay baruur ugu barato ayey macaluul ugu go'daa
The fox is likely to starve at the sight of a previous feast

Nimaan shaqeysan shaah waa ka xaaraan

He who does not toil will not be served at the dinner table (earnings are forbidden that he who doesn't work for it)

Fiqi tolkii kama janno tago
A pious man doesn't choose to go to paradise without his kinsmen

Falkooni waa feejignaan
Prevention is better than cure

Magaalo waxaa lagu joogaa maan kaa badan, maro kaa badan iyo maskax kaa badan
Urban life demands a logical mind, appropriate attire and rational intelligence

Qofna wuxuusan lahayn kuma baahi baxo
What is not one's never satisfies (unearned provisions never fully satisfy one's needs)

Aaddane eed ma waayo
Human beings are never without a fault

Dhibbaan eebo waa laga bogsadaa, dhaawac carrab Aaddanase lagama bogsado
One may recover from injuries ordained by fate, but to recover from the wagging tongue of men is harder

Laabi laba u la'
One cannot accommodate two conflicting thoughts at the same time (to exercise two opposing inner-thoughts together at the same time are difficult and confusing)

Qaniinyo, qaniinyaa kaa fujisa
Answer a bite with a bite (tit-for-tat)

Hor u cune dib uma cuno
He who uses up his share earlier, does not deserve another share later (one has to use his/her provisions wisely and economically)

Tuugo kula taali tabtaa ma weydo
Thieves in your household know where you are most vulnerable

Waayeel kaftan buu hadalkiisa ku bogtaa
An elder can make his/her point even with a joke

Qacda hore layga tegyaaba, qacday yeedhay
First impressions are most lasting

Kolka weylaha la helaa, lo'da la maalaa
When rogues fall out, honest men come into their own

Afeef hore lahow ama adkeysi dambe lahow
Speak out before hand or accept any consequences of your silence

Wax rag kaa gallay rako kaa gale
What is taken from you by men is like an object hanging from a high cliff

Hal diidaysaa geed ay ku xoqato ma weydo
A she-camel that is rejecting its calf will find an excuse under every tree

Hal libaax u jeeddaa ma godlato
A she-camel that senses a lion's near-presence never gets ready for milking

Wixii muuqdaa muhiim gala
What is visible is what is practicable (a positive result at hand is better than empty day dreams)

Uur lama xukmiyee, afbaa la xukmiyaa
One cannot easily gauge one's inner-most thoughts but can only judge one's words

Mukulaal minankeeda joogtaa miciyo libaax bay leedahay
A cat in its own den fancies itself as having the fangs of a lion (one's home is better and saver than anywhere else)

Hu'gaagu waa kula shir tagaa
Your outfit even accompanies you to a council meeting (the way one dresses reflects his/her character and fore-tells that person's future behavior; so it pays to be clean, elegant and well-looking at all times)

Afkii ba'ay yiri toobana wuu karaa
He who cries 'shucks' can also cry for repentance (means if one offends someone, he/she can also apologize to him/her if he/she wants to)

Wax aan calaf ahayn lama cuno, wax aan wed ahayna looma dhinto
No one eats what is not his/her provision and no one dies but from Death itself (you eat your share of life and will die when your predestined time of death comes)

Geesi Alle ma xiro
God does not throw obstacles in a brave man's path (the brave man always brings a quick and simple solution to all of his grudges and solves them either by word or by spear)

Qofna qawlkiisuu hadlaa, qorina qiiqiisuu baxaa
A man speaks his mind, and a piece of wood (or a gun) makes smoke in accordance to its calibre

Qaran qabiil laguma ahaado
Clanism does not beget a nation (a nation can prosper if it has a viable ideology and competent administration; and not by tribalism, nepotism and misguided idealism)

Nin aan talin jirin hadduu taliyo nin aan tegi jirin baa taga
When the unwise lead the council's deliberations, the wise must depart (the unwise spoil rightful council and may not accept corrections)

Nin walba halka bugtaa isagay balbashaa
Every man knows what hurts him the most

Shar u toog hay khayr wax kaama dhimmee
Be alert to trouble; goodness can't hurt you (while you are in good fortune, be prepared for the troubles that may dog you in the future)

Karti laawe degdeg buu door bidaa
The short cut is always the longest

Dad iyo duurba wax aadan filayn ayaa kaaga soo baxa
Both people and thickets may spring surprises on you

Tog wailba taagtiisuu rogmadaa, qof walbana tabartii bay qodaxi ugu tagtaa
Every river rolls with the force of its torrent and every thorn penetrates the foot relative to the weight of the walker

Rabbi ka baq iyo rag iska riix meel ma wada galaan
To worship God and be antagonistic to mankind; the two never go together

Ninna oogadiisa biyo kama hagrado
No man spares cooling water off his sweltering body (in the heat of day)

Sida aad doonayso haddii aad weydo sida aad ka badin weydo ayaa la yeelaa
If you cannot get your way, do what you can (flexibility saves more time and energy for its practictioner , so one has to be smart enough to look things from many angles with a wider scope and vision)

Doqon Alle taqaan lagama gar hello
Even a fool may win his case, as long as he believes in God (A fool who believes in God will never be defeated; as we know God helps one when he/she is helping by his or herself; but the fool who always makes mistakes and claims he/she did it because of God's will is a person with no understanding and is misleading the faith which he/she believes in and too difficult to deal with;

the dilemma is if he/she claims that a thing happened because of God's will you can't even quarrel with him/her because of that, so you will find yourself in a no- mans-land)

Hadday laabi meel dhacdo, indho wax ma arkaan
When the heart desires, the eyes are blind (heart leads and eyes follow)

Nebi Allow ninba afkii kugu ammaan
O' the Prophet of Allah; each man can only praise you to the extent of his eloquence (this points to differences in human language and to the extent each society uses language and how each and single person within that same community worships God)

Neef gawracani geedo kama waabto
A beast whose throat is slit does not avoid obstacles (if you have no hope, you have no choice either)

Nin aan dhididini ma dhergo
He, who does not sweat, does not get his fill

Miro barde duuduubkaa lagu liqaa
One should eat prunes in whole (problems between the people of respective relations are good to solve as a package instead of trying to know each and every thing of about them)

Nin shimbiro sabaayaa waraf kama sanqariyo
A bird hunter should not rattle his sling

Run iyo roob midna lagama raysto
One never gets enough of either truth or rain

Seddex Illaah waa karaa mase yeelo: Allow guursan maayee hay gablamin; Allow xoogsan maayee xoolo i sii; iyo Allow cibaadeysan maayee hay cadaabin
God never grants the following three wishes: even if I don't marry, bless me with off-spring; even if I don't work, please favor

me with riches; and even if I fail to worship, please do not condemn me to hell-fire

Waa baryaaba barakadii leh
Every new dawn brings its own blessing

Adduunyo orod laguma gaaro
You cannot catch the world in a wild pursuit (one has to take it easy and plan prudently)

Nin aan waxa jooga ka talini waxa soo socda kama taliyo
A man who cannot counsel about the present will not counsel about the future (means if you cannot see the present reality on the ground there is no way you can think or see the future)

Rag talo kama dhammaato
Men never get enough of advice (there are new things to ponder always in the human mind based on different situations and times)

Talo iskuma kaa sheegto
The right counsel is seldom evident (you don't know what will happen so you cannot always arm yourself as what to, because there are alawys new problems and blessings on every single given day; so, you have to cope with all these things with caution and tackle each problem separately and solve it when it comes; you cannot trust the chance)

Talo ayuu rag isku dhaafaa
The right counsel separates equal men into different categories (someone with good counsel and intellectuality always is much saver and much more advanced than one with bad counsel)

Rag waa talo keen ama waa talo raac
Men are either counselors or followers (everyone cannot be a counselor; few men advises and the rest heed; that means all men are not bosses but some lead and the rest must follow)

Nin aan hadlin habartii wax ma siiso
He who doesn't speak up, even his mother doesn't feed him

Nin aan wed dilin waran ma dilo
The spear doesn't kill one who isn't killed by death

Booraan hadimo ha qodin haddii aad qoddana ha dheereyn ku dhici doontidaana ma ogide
Don't dig a hole of deceit, and if you must dig it don't dig it too deep for you never know who may fall into it – it could even be you!

War la qabaa xiiso ma leh
There can be no excitement about old news (the news in hand has no interest; if someone brings news that has been already received then it will not create any more interest for the designated party)

Garba gar baa la tusaa
Match a verdict with a verdict (every verdict has the same characteristics to a another verdict, so matching them is a wise idea)

Nin intaad ka baqayso labadeed buu kaa baqaa
Every man may fear you twice as much as you fear him

Gacantii qaad-qaad barata gummudkaa dhaqdhaqaaqa
A hand that steals ends up in amputation (a stealing hand never stops even after amputation)

Nin dayro badan degel lalama dego
Don't be a neighbor to a miser (don't be a neighbor to a man who always minimizes his wealth in the same encampment)

Hooyo baalkeeday ilmaha ku korisaa
A mother raises children in her lap

Talo aan la gorfeyn geed lalama tago

One should not bring to the council-tree a position not aforethought (inconclusive counsel is not a good thing to take to an assembly)

Doqontu halka lagu qalayey qoorta dhigataa
A fool places his neck on the chopping block (don't ever take uncessary risks)

Il ibtileysan yaa belaayo tilmaanta
Those who only seek for faults find nothing else

Oodi qaadid iyo jiidid waa isla xero geyn
It doesn't matter whether one carries or pulls a thorn-bush to build a corral

Timaha qaar madal baa lagu xiiraa qaarna maad baa lagu xiiraa
Part of one's hair may be shaved publicly, while the rest is shaved privately (means all words don't need to be expressed publicly, everything has its prerequisites and must be treated accordingly by its nature)

Liin qura ayaa liimo badan qurmisa
One rotten lemon can spoil the whole (always one has to separate things in categories to safeguard the rest)

Dagaal nin aan aqoon baa ku orda
A man who doesn't know about war is likely the one who rushes to it

Rag hortii lama cawdo
Don't lament in the presence of men—if you're a man!

Gaashaan-qaad ma habaabo
A young man who can bear arms does not go astray (in the Somali's view the young man which this proverb is applying to is the twelve year old lad; and it means at that age he has to manage things smoothly and must take responsibilities on his shoulders)

Ragow naago ogow, naagowna rag ogaada
O' men, care for your women dearly; and you women, attend to your men's needs

Falaari gil-gilasho kaagama harto
A barbed arrow does not fall from your flesh by shaking it (means whatever shame or scandal one causes will always remain as unique identities whether one denies it or not; so, better be cautious before you acquire ill-rebute)

Caydu dadka ayay kugu dirtaa kaamase celiso
Insolence creates enemies for you but it never defends you

Nin kaa xoog badani hortaabuu xanaaqaa
A man mightier than you is more likely to get offended first (because he thinks that he can defeat you easily if hostility erupts between you)

Milil dushii lama dhayo
It's not a good idea to treat a sore spot superficially (means problems deserve to be treated as deep as they are instead of engaging in pseudo-medication)

Nin yiri waxaa ma arag inteeduusan jirin, nin yiri waxaa ma cunina baahideeduusan arag
He who said, "I never saw that" is inexperienced, and he who said, "I never ate that" has never been in need

Martidaa waa intaad soori kartaa, magantaana waa intaad bixin kartaa
Your guests are as much as you can host, and your refugees are as much as you can protect

Qaran dumay qayladii badan
The defeated can only protest vociferously (when unrest erupts in a nation, then the laments of its people can be heard far and wide)

Naf bugta boqol u talisay

A sick person obtains advice from all (this proverb has a same wisdom to the one above!)

Seddex tol la'aan baa leh: nin hurdoon la kicin; nin haroon la sugin; iyo nin hadloon la maqal
Three end up without kinsmen: don't awake for he who is asleep; don't wait for he who is tardy; and don't listen to he who talks

Illaahay ma naxee wuu naxariistaa
God may not show concern, but He is capable of compassion

Ballan fiid jarmaado arooryuu leedahay
Preparations in the evening brings about a setting-out in the early morning (an entrust at night brings about a setting-out in the early morning)

Dhaan loo kala eg
A water caravan sets apart its own men (every person matches with his/her profession)

Bahal higlo af-qurun kuma kala tagto kumana wada joogto
Carnivorous animals neither stay together nor disperse on account of rotten mouths (every society has its differences but always there are more important commonalities, which make them to co-exist and live together to defend their virtues and sovereignty; therefore the common interest overcomes the personal and particular issues)

Ilko abeeso hoostay ka xiriiraan
An adder's teeth have a hidden truce (this indicates the importance of unity)

Intaad dhaqantahaa la dhawrsadaa
Be clean and careful while you are still respected

Nin been yaqaan waa nin fal yaqaan
A liar is like a magician

Xagaagii tegey xoortii laga dhamay iyo xusuus baa geela lagu xero geeyaa
The milk drunk from it during the rainy season are the fond memories of the camel's home-coming (not a proverb but it has its own preservation as a daily use wisdom)

Faq fagaaruu tagaa
Whispered secrets sometimes get exposed (confidential speech sometimes comes out to the public; means as long as you tell something out from your heart sooner or later that secret will come out by itself and there is no way you can control these secrets after you utter them)

Nin laba jir u fuushan yahay lama xanto
Don't gossip about a man who is carrying a two-year-old lad (no body should be ignored, so you have to respect even youngsters and keep your words safely with dignity)

Walaalkaa wiil u lahow, wiilkaagana walaal u lahow
Have a son for your brother, and a brother for your son (men are not always easy to deal with; so it is safe to have a son who will defend you from your own brothers and having another son is enough to make you even saver from each of your sons who may be a threat to you, just in case)

Bakayle intuu bur ku jiruu bur kale daydaydaa
A rabbit looks for a new sanctuary while still in a safe place (this is about good management; so, one has to plan the next positive step while in a safe and sound place)

Nin tolkii ka tegey oo taakuleysta la waa, nin xajkii tegey oo xoolo keena la waa, nin xabaal galay oo soo xayaaba la waa
No one ever sees a man who succeeds without his kinsmen; or a man who comes from pilgrimage with a bundle of wealth; or one who ever returns from his burial place after death

Intay nabadi joogtaa ninba laba nin le'egyahay

All men are equal in peace time (every man thinks that he is braver than others while there is peace)

Gol ey baa lagu sahanshaa, xasna ul baa lagu sahanshaa
A dog is best in searching the woods and a stick is best in searching thickets (this is the equivalent of the same proverb, "look before you leap," that we have mentioned somewhere else in this chapter earlier)

Carruuri waa muslim iyo gaalo hadba kii lagu daraa
Children are what you make them

Nin aan wax aqoon qaanso gurgurkeed ayaa wax loo saaraa, nin wax yaqaanse daaqsin geel baa wax loo mariyaa
Learning makes the wise wiser, but the fool more foolish

Iimaan waa uur muggii
Enough is as good as a feast

Shaki yaqiin uga bax
Clear your doubts by seeking the truth (clarify and prove your suspicions and don't let suspense dictate your life and your mental stability so you better find the reality behind your suspicions and solve it as early as possible and never allow yourself to live with the darkness of your doubts)

Looma garaabo dhurwaa calooshu ka soo jeedo ilaa aad aragto kii kale
Never feel sympathy to a hyena with its entrails hanging out until you discover who caused him the injury (if you rush to judgment, it's possible to cause injustice if the other party has already passed away because of a damage inflicted by the present victim; so help those who are presently in need and hold your verdict till you meet the other party)

Walaalkaa gar iyo gardarraba ugu hiilli
Give your support to your brother whether he's the victim or the offender (if he is the victim defend him and restore his rights, and

if he's the victimizing part hold him and counsel him to stop the aggression and if he refuses to heed your advice punish him accordingly; this resembles the other proverbs about justice)

Quraanjo aruurtay mulac way jiiddaa
When ants band together they can drug even a mighty lizard (this is about unity and its success)

Guur waa seddex: dab dab saar; bari dab saar; iyo bari bari saar
There are three manners of marriage: fire on fire (between two who are poor); fat on fire (between rich and poor); and fat on fat (between two riches)

Haddii aad ammaan rabtana u dhimo, haddii aad cay rabtana u guurso
If you want to be praised die for it, but if you want to be insulted marry for it (when you die people remember all about your strengths but when you marry they discover all your weaknesses)

Biyo meel godan bay iskugu tagaan
Water seeks the lowest ground (water flows together at the lowest point)

Jiilaal iyo ninkii way legdamayaan oo hadba kay naagtu raacdo ayaa adkaada
A man and hard times are often locked in a struggle, and the ultimate winner always is the one that a woman supports (women are the best friend of men and whomever they stand by is the one who succeeds the most)

Xantaada xiinkeedaa kuu baxa
You can often hear the sound of a gossip perpetrated against you (you become aware of the gossip against you, whether you know or not its original source)

Xalaal iftiin baa la qashaa

The permissible can be shared in broad day light (legal things can be shared in public without fear; but illegal things need to be hidden and shared privately with fear)

Xaajo nin aan ogayni indhuhuu ka riddaa
An ignorant fool can often cast doubt on a just cause (one has to understand an affair before he participates)

Doqoni seddex bay la weynaataa; wax cun, wax dhac iyo wax dil
Fools prosper by means of the following credo; eating every thing it sees, robbing whoever it finds, and killing anyone weaker than her

Dad wax-yar-tare mooyee wax-ma-tare ma leh
There are no completely useless persons, but there are plenty of do-littles

Ruqo geel oo ninkii lahaa daba jiidayaa ma kacdo
An old she-camel whose rightful owner is holding her down by the tail never rises (a problem whose victims are not happy with its solution will never bear any fruits of success and will remain unsolvable)

Run iyo beeni kala raad leh
Truth and lie have different footprints

Rag shir lagama daayo, arina shiro lagama daayo, lo'na shinsi lagama daayo
Men never tire of assemblies; goats are never safe from slaughtering and cattle from milking expectations

Saaxiibkaa ama kuu sahan ahaa ama kuu sabab ahaa
Your friend can either lead you to a safe haven or to a place of danger

Saaxiibkaa mar ku diin, mar ku dayo, marna ka dar
Amaze your friend once, once imitate him, and once over-shadow him

Dhool bari ka hooraa dhaan loo negeeyaa
When you see rain-bearing clouds gathering in the eastern horizon, let your water caravan stay home

Caanihii daata dabadoodaa la qabtaa
Try to save what remains of spilling milk

Col hortiibaa la hub sameystaa
Get your weapons ready before the enemy arrives (to be cautious is always important)

Col ku galay cabsi kugu reeb
An enemy attack may leave you in terror (an invading army may leave behind fear; whenever a problem occurs its negative impact is always visible and its uncertainties are unbearable later on)

Col naago ka kacay iyo caro nirig ka kacday midkoodna ma qaboobo
Animosity caused by women and anger caused by a camel foal seldom cool off (Somalis value dearly the importance of women and camels which are the life-line of that society and any wrongs towards them may erupt the inferno of animosities and result in a long conflict and many painful scars)

Gacan-qaad aan laguu ogayn is war baa la yiraahdaa
An ignored hand-shake may cause you later grief

Geed walba xaabo gubtaa way hoostaal
There are enough fire sticks under any tree to burn it down (every person has his/her own problems; therefore there is no one who is immune from troubles, so one should not entertain such a thought)

Fuley xantii ma mooga
A coward is seldom unaware of plots hatched against him (every human being knows his/her own weaknesses)

Fari tog dheer bay kula xushaa

A Stream can carry you to a water-shed (your minimal misbehaving can cause you a bigger and more dangerous risk)

Keligi cune kelidii buu dhintaa
Who eats alone dies alone (if one is selfish, then there will be no help available for him/her when needed)

Geeriyi nin aadan aqoon iyo geeljir bay ku fiican tahay
Death is best deserved by strangers and camel-herders (if one tells you the death of someone you know that news affects you, but if they talk about the death of someone you don't know, then your sorrow is brief)

Nin ay habari dhashay hal ma seegi waayo
There is no man who can't make a mistake (everyone can make a mistake but the best of all is he who corrects his misdeeds)

Madax aadan lahayn miyirkiisa la isma saaro
One cannot possess someone else's wisdom

Haween quruxna ha ku raacin foolxumana ha uga tegin
Don't choose women for beauty and don't dislike them for ugliness (choose one who will provide you love and dignity with a strong economic base, who is born of good parents and has a noble ancestral line)

Badow magaalo galay waa dameer masaajid galay
A Bedouin who enters a town is like a donkey that enters a mosque

Aan wada hadalno waa aan heshiino
'Let us talk' means 'let us solve our problems'

Libaax laba raqood lagama wada kiciyo
Don't make the mistake of chasing a lion from his kill twice

Waran kugu soo laaban doona lama tuuro

Don't throw a spear that may boomerang on you (never throw a spear that will kill you back; during the battle if you throw a spear you have to throw it precisely, otherwise you make it easy for your enemy to throw that same spear back and kill you)

Wax is weydiin ma xumee wax is weydaarin baa daran
A request is reasonable, but deception is unacceptable

Hadal waa murti iyo yoon-yoon
Speech is either substantive or else nonsensical (the whole of speech is divided into these categories, so it's better that one choose the wise one and keep the non-sense part of it in his/her heart)

Haddii hammaddaadu kuu been sheegto, tabartaada ayaa kuu run sheegta
If your desire lies to you, your ability tells you the truth (if you try to do something that is hard to do, then you can still try to do it but your strength dictates as much as you can do and you can't do more than you could do)

Dagaal ha ku degdegin, kan sokeeyana haba deyin, haddiise rag ku deyn waayo, ha u daymo la'aan; soor ha ku degdegin, tan fagaarana haba deyin, haddaanse ceebi kaa raacayn, ha u daymo la'aan; haween ha ku degdegin, dharaarna haba deyin, haddiise dad ku baaqanayo, ha u daymo la'aan.
Don't rush to war, and don't even mind your kinsmen's quarrels, but if men will not leave you alone, don't be unmindful; don't rush to food, and don't even mind if it's in the mist of a crowd, but if its not shaming you, don't miss it; don't rush into seducing women, and don't even mind it even if it is in broad day light, but if they're still productive, don't miss that chance (this lengthily proverb indicates the importance of balancing one's self and how wise it is to be cautious before commencing anything)

Awr kala guurtay ma xumee, uur kala guuray baa daran

It is not bad thing if caravans separate; but it is only bad if they forsake each other (departing hearts from each other are the most dangerous)

Wax badso wax beel bay leedahay
Too much greed leads to disappointment

Billaysin bir ka adag
One's first impression upon birth is even more unbreakable than a bar of metal

Geel kurus baa lagu oggaa, rag xaajaa lagu oggaa, haweena xishood baa lagu oggaa
Camels have humps, men have issues (to solve), and women are endowed with modesty

Af-maal ma iisho
A man with a sense of humor is never at a loss for words of action (An eloquent mouth never vanishes; an intelligent orator's ideas and wisdoms live on, even after his death; and that is the message that this proverb is indicating or shedding light on)

Gacal isma ciriirsho
Beloved ones never cramp/oppress to one another

Murtidu waa hodantinnimo, oraahdeedna waa deeq
Wisdom is a treasure

Maangaab meel ka dhac waa leeyahay, meel u dhacse ma laha
Many find fault without an end, and yet do nothing at all to mend

Ayaanle waa eedeysan yahay
Fortune favors fools

Goof maran malab shinniyeed kama guratid
Never a rose without thorns

Hilib geel lagama dhergo ee waa laga qaraaraa

Too much of one thing is good for nothing

Ninkaad barashadiisa rabto jid la mar, jediin la cun ama jabad la deg
Never trust a man or a woman, until you know the worse of them

Laba daran mid dooro
Of the two evils choose the less

Mar I dage Allaha dago, mar labaad I dagase, anaa dagan
If a man deceives me once, shame on him, if twice shame on me

Nin aan ku aqooni kuma temmedo
He who does not know you, does not value you

Ninba wuxuu doonuu garaadkeeda leeyahay
The wish is father of thought

Qofkaad barashadiisa rabto saaxiibkiisaa la bartaa
Whom you want to know better, you have to know his friend

Quraanjo arruurtay mulac way jiiddaa
When the webs of ant join, they can pull a lizard

Quud aan jirin qoryo looma gurto
Never count a provision that is not in your possession

Haruub walba haantiisaa ka weyn
Every lid/cover is always bigger by its jar

Wixii nin la toosani nin la tuur leh
One man's gravy is another man's poison (what is pleasing to one person may not be pleasing to another

Qosol lagaaga dambeeyaa qosol ma'ahan
He who laughs last, laughs best (the person who succeeds in making the last move has the most fun)

Nin waliba gurigi gaado ku leh
A man's house is his castle (every one has his/her best character and personality at his/her house)

Ninkaad barashadiisa rabto jidiin la cun; jid la mar ama jabad la deg
The man you want to know his best, you must share a provision with him; go travel with him or become with his neighbor

Waa la doogine yaan la dacaroon
Abundant of prosperity will arrive so one has not to stain his dignity (dignify your name high just in case the good days come back)

Bahal ceeriin ma daayo ninna caadadi ma baajo
Carnivores never stop eating fleshes and men never forbid their customs

Maangaab meel ka dhac waa leeyahay, meel u dhacse ma laha
Many find fault without an end, and yet do nothing at all to mend

Il ibtileysan yaa belaayo tilmaanta
Those who only seek for faults find nothing else

Garawshiiyo waa geel siin
A fault confessed is half redressed

War jiraaba cakaaruu iman
For every prophecy there is a fixed time

Habar fadhidaa legdin la fududyahay
Lookers on see most of the game

Haddii aad been sheegayso, been run u eg baa la sheegaa
If you want to lie, make it as true

Wixii caloosha kaaga jira carrabkaa kaa xada
What the heart thinks the tongue speaks

Ruux waliba wuxuu dhiteystuu dhaxalkeeda leeyahay
Vice its own punishment, virtue its own reward

Jaallahaa kuma jebiyo
A friend in need is a friend indeed

Geedjoog gartii wuu yaqaan
Experienced man is like a great teacher (an experienced person never lose his/her verdict)

Xikmad la'aan caqligu wuu xaalufaa
Manners maketh man, wisdom great men

Doqoni xarkaha lagu xirxirayo xusuladay ku sidataa
Give a fool a rope and he will hang himself

Tuhun waa sed
Suspicion is the bare of friendship

Duqsigii biyo ku dabbaal bartaa fuud buu ku gubtaa
Flies are easier caught with honey than with vinegar

Gaashaanqaad ma habaabo
A young lad who's able to bear a spear never lose his way

Bakhtiwareen waa xaaraan
Speak only good about the dead

Oodo dhacameed siday u kala sarreeyaan baa loo kala guraa
First come, first served

Barasho yari waa bil seddexaad
Little knowledge is dangerous

Ballandarro waa diindarro
A man without promise is a man without faith

Chapter IV
Selected & Useful Foreign Sayings

Myth, fable, legend and history intertwine in the proverb, thus it is said that behind every adage lies a tale. And when this tale has been forgotten, lost in the mist of time, another tale is often invented to fit the proverb. Spanish Proverbs, Idioms & Slang, by Jean & Susan Serrano. P.71

- -

Knowledge is like a garden, if it is not cultivated, it will not be harvested – African Proverb

A good name is rather to be chosen than great riches - Hebrwew biblical proverb

A soft answer turneth away wrath - Hebrwew biblical proverb

Pride goeth before destruction and a haughty spirit before a fall - Hebrwew biblical proverb

Hope deferred maketh the heart sick - Hebrew biblical proverb

A lone runner says he has legs (runs fast) - Kenyan proverb

Make hay while the sun shines (take advantage of an opportunity to do something) - English proverb

A tractor driver doesn't fear dust - Kenyan proverb and is equivalent to a Somali proverb which is saying 'A wet man need not avoid water'

Strike while the iron is hot (act at the best possible time) - English proverb

All monkeys can not hung on the same branch - Kenyan proverb

An orphaned calf licks its own back - Kenyan proverb

Chances comes to those who know what they want – English proverb

The best remedy for dispute is to discuss it – English proverb and is equivalent to Somali proverb which says 'Let us talk means let us solve our problems'

Big talkers won't be your in-laws long - Kenyan proverb

He who has not carried your burden does not know what it weights – English proverb and is equivalent to Somali proverb which says 'Two who have stayed separately in distances may have no knowledge of each other's fortunes (or misfortunes)'

Cross the river before you insult the crocodile – English proverb

Give to the earth and the earth will give to you – English proverb

Speak silver, reply gold – English proverb

Leave a good name behind in case you return – English proverb and is equivalent to Somali proverb which says 'Since you will not live forever better leave a good name behind'

Water is never tired of flowing – English proverb

A small house will hold a hundred friends – English proverb and is equivalent to Somali proverb which says 'Beloved ones never cramp/oppress to one another'

The way to a man's heart is through his stomach (the way to gain a man's love is by preparing food that he enjoys) - English proverb

A bow-legged person does not hunt antelope - Kenyan proverb

Does a man set up a plantation without a wife? - Ganda proverb, Uganda, Kenya

When in Rome do as the Romans do (when traveling, follow the customs of the local people) - English proverb

No child should be babied while another is offered to the hyena to bite - Kenyan proverb

One in the woodpile does not laugh at the one in the fire - Kenyan proverb

Do good; you will find good – English proverb

Forgiveness from the heart is better than a box of gold – English proverb

Curiosity killed the cat (it is dangerous to be curious) - English proverb

Only a medicine man gets rich by sleeping - Kenyan proverb

Regular work tires a woman but totally wrecks a man - Kenyan proverb

Don't bite off more than you can chew ((don't assume more responsibilty than you can handle; don't be overconvident) - English proverb

The possessor may become dispossessed - Kenyan proverb

Your mother is still your mother, though her legs are small - Chewa proverb, Malawi

Don't bite the hand that feeds you (don't hurt someone who takes care of you) - English proverb

Two roads overcame the hyena "No one can serve two masters...You cannot serve God and wealth," - Swahili, Eastern Africa and Luhya proverbs, Kenya

A word in the heart does not win "open your mouth in behalf of the dumb, and for the rights of the destitute." - Kikuyu proverb, Kenya

Don't count your chickens before they're hatched (don't plan on the successful results of something until those results actually occur) - English proverb

Traveling is learning "he travels among the peoples of foreign lands to learn what is good and evil." - Shona Ethnic Group, Zimbabwe and Kikuyu Ethnic Group, Kenya

To be hated by a human being is not to be hated by God "do not be afraid of those who kill the body but cannot kill the soul; rather be afraid of the one who can destroy both soul and body in Gehenna." - Kikuyu proverb, Kenya

The proof is in the pudding (the only way to judge something is to try it) - English proverb

He whose seeds have not germinated does not put down the seed container "work out your salvation with fear and trembling." - Kikuyu proverb, Kenya

Possession is nine-tenths of the law (the person who possesses something has the strongest claim to owning it) - English proverb

Two guests cannot be entertained satisfactorily at the same time "No one can serve two masters. You cannot serve God and mammon." - Kikuyu proverb, Kenya

One person is thin porridge or gruel; two or three people are a handful of stiff cooked corn meal "Two are better than one...A threefold cord is not quickly broken." - Kuria Ethnic Group, Kenya, Tanzania and Ngoreme Ethnic Group, Tanzania

Nothing hurts like the truth (it is painful to discover an unpleasant truth about oneself) - English proverb

To laugh at a person with a defective eye while you hide your own defects "Why do you see the speck in your neighbor's eye, but do not notice the log in your own eye?" - Sukuma proverb, Tanzania

No news is good news (if one does not hear the outcome of a situation, that outcome must be positive) - English proverb

What goes into the stomach is not lasting "Do you not see that whatever goes into a person from outside cannot defile, since it enters, not the heart but the stomach, and goes out into the sewer." - Sukuma proverb, Tanzania

Might makes right (the stronger of two opponents will always control the situation) - English proverb

Hindsight is better than foresight (people see and understand things more clearly after they've happened than before they've happened) - English proverb

Suppression of hunger leads to death - Luhya proverb, Kenya

Only someone else can scratch your back - Luhya proverb, Kenya

Lightning never strikes twice in the same place (the same misfortune won't necessarily happen twice to the same person) - English proverb

The eyes of the in-laws ignore what they have seen - Luhya proverb - Kenya

The broken plate cannot be rejoined - Luhya proverb, Kenya

When it rains, it pours (good and bad things tend to happen in groups - English proverb?

The grass is always greener on the other side of the fence (another place or situation always appears to be better than your own) - English proverb

The blame of the antelope is on the hunter - Luhya proverb Kenya

The greedy one swells the stomach - Luhya proverb, Kenya

Good things come in small packages (small containers can hold objects of great value) - English proverb

The fire burns the fire maker - Luhya proverb, Kenya

You only make a bridge where there is a river - Luhya proverb, Kenya

The bigger they are, the harder they fall (the more important someone is, the more severe are the consequences of his or her failure) - English proverb

We can't depend on one brave man - Luhya proverb, Kenya

The best things in life are free (the things that give a person the most happiness don't cost anything) - English proverb

The lame knows how to fall - Luhya proverb, Kenya

Blind belief is dangerous - Luhya proverb, Kenya

Bad news travels fast (reports of problems and misfortune spread quickly) - English proverb

Bad dancing does not break an engagement - Luhya proverb, Kenya

After the feast comes the reckoning (people must always pay the price of their excesses) - English proverb

A Champion bull starts from birth - Luhya proverb, Kenya

You reap what you sow (the amount of effort you put into something determines how much you will get out of it) - English proverb and is equivalent to Somali proverb which says "At age sixty you reap the fruit of the tree that you have sown at age twenty (the amount of effort you put into something while young and energetic determines how much you will get out of it at a later age)"

The pillar of the world is hope - Kanuri proverb, Nigeria

He who marries a real beauty is seeking trouble - Accra proverb, Ghana

You have to take the good with the bad (you must accept disappointment along with success) - English proverb

The young can't teach traditions to the old - Yoruba proverb, Nigeria

There is no medicine against old age - Accra proverb, Ghana

One good turn deserves another (a favor should be repaid with another favor) - English & Somali proverb and equivalent to Somali proverb which says "You milk a beast for they who milk for you (generosity works both ways, so you must be generous to your helpers when they are in need)"

That man's a fool - whose sheep flees twice - Oji proverb and equivalent to Somali proverb which says "He who deceives me once, may Allah deceive him, but if the same man deceives me again, I deserve to be deceived"

When your mouth stumbles, it's worse than feet - Oji proverb

Love makes the world go round (when people show respect and consideration for one another, the world is a better place) – Anonymous

Hold a true friend with both hands - Kanuri proverb, Nigeria

A book is like a garden carried in the pocket – English proverb

One does not love if one does not accept from others - Kanuri proverb, Nigeria

Rising early makes the road short - Wolof proverb, Senegal

Haste makes waste (when one hurries too much, one is likely to do a poor job and have to waste time doing it over) - English proverb

It is better to walk than curse the road - Wolof proverb, Senegal

If there is cause to hate someone, the cause to love has just begun - Wolof, Senegal

Children will hate all those who give all things to them - Wolof proverb, Senegal

The teeth of a man serve as a fence - Wolof proverb, Senegal

We add wisdom to knowledge - Kalenjin proverb, Kenya

A hyena cannot smell its own stench - Kalenjin proverb, Kenya and is equivalent to Somali proverb which says "An elephant doesn't see the gadfly on its back but can easily see the gadfly on another elephant's back (people see each other's negativities; but it's much harder for some one to see his/her own faults)"

Do not follow a person who is running away - Kalenjin proverb, Kenya

We should put out fire while it is still small -Kalenjin proverb, Kenya

Water can not be forced uphill - Kalenjin proverb, Kenya

Man proposes, and God disposes/decides - English proverb

The rest on the road does not end the journey – English proverb

The peapole know each other better on a journey – Sechuana proverb and is equivalent to Somali proverb which says "The man you want to know his best, you must share a provision with him; go travel with him or become with his neighbor"

A crime eats its own child – Sechuana proverb

A sorcerer has no distinctive color – Sechuana proverb

Let rats shoot arrows at each other - Sudanese proverb

You suffer from smoke produced by the firewood you fetched yourself - Luhya proverb, Kenya

Be on the alert, like the red ant that moves with its claws wide open - Ugandan proverb

Instruction in youth is like engraving in stones - Berber proverb, North Africa

To be happy in one's home is better than to be a chief -Yoruba proverb, Nigeria

The elephant never gets tired of carrying its tusks - Vai proverb, Liberia

By coming and going, a bird weaves its nest - Ashanti proverb, Ghana

Down here or up there, God ordains - Spanish proverb

It is better that trials come to you in the beginning and you find peace afterwards than that they come to you at the end - Kiganda proverb, Democradic Republic of Congo

Silence is also speech – English proverb

You are sitting in peace (unharmed): as the nose of a cow that feeds among thorn trees and shows no scars - Kiganda proverb, Democradic Republic of Congo

Charity begins at home (one should take care of one's own family, friends, or fellow citizens before helping other people) - English proverb

The rainmaker who doesn't know what he is doing will be found out by the lack of clouds - Kiganda proverb, Democradic Republic of Congo

One who is crazy for meat hunts buffalo (the most dangerous game animal) - Luganda proverb, Uganda and is equivalent to Somali proverb which says "Someone who doesn't know the true nature of a lion may chase him to recover a stolen ewe (it's easy for an inexperienced man to take all kinds of risks without considering the consequences)"

Whom God loves well, his dog will have a litter of piglets (this indicates that a person's good luck depends on God's will) - Spanish proverb

The one who says, "My home is peaceful," buys millet (for brewing beer). [Meaning: a foolish act -- when the beer is drunk, the peace of the home will be upset) - Anonymous
A bird in the hand is worth two in the bush (something you already have is better than something you might get) - English proverbs and is equivalent to Somali proverb which says "Never

discard fruits in your pocket for fruits in some tree (something you already have is better than something you might later get)"

God's rain falls even on the witch - Fipa proverb, Tanzania

One who sees something good must narrate it - Ganda proverb, Uganda

Better safe than sorry (it is better to choose a safe course of action than a risky one that could lead to regret), English & Somali proverbs

To be praised is to be lost - Kikuyu proverb - Kenya

The one chased away with a club comes back, but the one chased away with kihooto (reason) does not - Kikuyu proverb, Kenya

He who refuses to obey cannot command - Kikuyu proverb, Kenya

Better late than never (it's better to do something late than not to do it at all) - English proverb

If one is roasting two potatoes, one of them is bound to get charred - Kikuyu proverb, Kenya

Goodness gets a seat, (explanation: good people will be shown favors and will live longer) - Igala proverb, Nigeria

My husband is a drummer; God gave him to me and I love as he is (as God gave him to me) - Spanish proverb

The frog does not run in the daytime for nothing - Igbo proverb, Nigeria

Actions speak louder than words (people's actions are more convincing than their words are) - English proverb

Do they prepare leather (for a battle shield) the day they fight? - Zar proverb, Nigeria

The cock crows, the idle person grumbles - Yoruba proverb, Nigeria

Doing one's best drives away regret – English proverb

A home without a mother is a desert - Eritrean proverb

Love is blind (one sees no faults in the person one loves) - English proverb

A camel does not joke about the hump on another camel - Guinea proverb

When an elephants fight, it is the grass that suffers - Kikuyu proverb, Kenya

Elderliness is not a disease, but richness is - Kiganda proverb, Democradic Republic of Congo

Imitation is the sincerest form of flattery (trying to be like some one is the most genuine way of praising that person) - English proverb

When others have received, you may also receive, because God is always present - Burundian proverb

Those who respect the elderly pave their own road toward success - African proverb - Anonymous

The tracks of the elephant cancel those of the antelope - Duala proverb, Cameroon

He who has drunk from the waters of Africa will drink again - Arabian proverb

The illness that has no cure, not even the priest (there are no cures for ill fate) - Spanish proverb

If you raise your hands (in adoration and prayer) to God, God will hear your prayer - Egyptian proverb

Foolishness often proceeds wisdom – English proverb

A friend who shares is a friend who cares (a true friend unselfishly shares what he or she has) - English proverb

If you are a flag follow the wind - Swahili proverb

The wise man's promises are like dew on the field - Nilotic proverb

The goat eats the grass where it is tied - Bamoun proverb, Cameroon

A friend in need is a friend indeed (a true friend will help you in a time of trouble) - English proverb

There is no hiding place on the water surface - Balari proverb

The villager who always complains and is never satisfied with anything is like an annoying flea on the foot - Nilotic proverb

Wind makes more noise among the trees - Kikuyu proverb, Kenya

Familiarity breeds contempt (when you know people well you will discover their waeknesses and you may come to scorn them) - English proverb

Proverbs are the daughters of experience - Sierra Leone

He who does not travel will not know the value of men - Berber proverb, North Africa and is equivalent to Somali proverb which says "He who has not traveled has no understanding (travel enhances one's experience and wisdom)"

God helps those who help themselves - Spanish proverb

In the eyes of its mother, every beetle is a gazelle - Moroccan proverb

Blood is thicker than water (members of the same family share stronger ties with each other than they do with others) - English proverb

People are wonderful and strange - Ibo proverb, Nigeria

A mother of twins must have a belly - Kundu proverb, Cameroon and is equivalent to Somali proverb which says "Every lid/cover is always bigger by its jar"

Absence makes the heart grow fonder (people often feel more affectionate toward each other when they are apart) - English proverb

It is a child that gives the parents the highest status - Ibo proverb, Nigeria

Beauty is in the eye of the beholder (what seems ordinary or ugly to one person might seem beautiful to another) - English proverb

Everyone knows the old woman's name, yet everyone calls her great-grandmother - Mamprusi proverb, Burkina Faso
You can't change your destiny - Aja-fon proverb, Benin

When a person is given a name, his spirits accept it - Ibo proverb, Nigeria

It is children that make relations - Ibo proverb, Nigeria

A bad name is ominous - Sotho proverb, Lesotho

When the cat's away the mice will play (some people will misbehave when they are not being watched) - English proverb

Give birth to children; you'll be pregnant with worries - Ovambo proverb, Namibia

To bear a girl is to bear a problem - Tigrinya proverb, Ethiopia and Eritrea

When the music changes, so does the dance - Hausa proverb, West Africa

Variety is the spice of life (differences and changes make life enjoyable) - English proverb

The custom of a country embarrasses the king - Amhara proverb, Ethiopia

To observe the taboos is to be alive - Ibo proverb, Nigeria

However far the stream flows, it never forgets its source - Yoruba proverb, Nigeria

There's no fool like an old fool (a foolish act seems even more foolish when performed by an older person, who should have a lot of wisdom) - English proverb

Go back and fetch what was left behind - Akan proverb, Ghana

If you find locals frying their eyes, fry yours also - Nyanja proverb, Malawi

May the sun smile upon you - Kalenjin of Kenya blessings, Kenya

Remember, after the storm there will be a rainbow - Nilotic proverb

When the webs of the spider join, they can trap a lion - Ethiopian proverb and is equivalent to Somali proverb which says "when the webs of ant join, they can pull a lizard"

There's more than one way to skin a cat (there are many ways to achieve a goal) - English proverb

When your finger is in pain, your sight is not lazy - Ekonda proverb, Democradic Republic of Congo

Disease and disasters come and go like rain, but health is like the sun that illuminates the entire village - Luo proverb, Kenya

Good actions are nourishment for youths, much more than words - North African proverb

There is no honor among thieves (one dishonest person cannot trust another) - English & Somali proverbs

The name is the spririt - Lala proverb, Democradic Republic of Congo

Each thing has its moment - Bambara proverb, Mali, Niger

A child is hard to come by - Ibo proverb, Nigeria

The spirit is willing, but the flesh is weak (a person's body is not always as strong as his or her mind) - English proverb
Children are the pleasure of the earth - Yoruba proverb, Nigeria

The state of the house must be considered before naming a child - Yoruba proverb, Nigeria

Do not sew a dress for the baby before the child is born - Tanzanian proverb and is equivalent to Somali proverb which says "never count a provision that is not in your possession"

The man who stumbles on richness names his son Olaniyonu ("riches entail problems") - Yoruba proverbb, Nigeria

One man's gravy is another man's poison (what is pleasing to one person may not be pleasing to another) - English & Somali proverb

Many births, many burials - Kikuyu proverb, Kenya

They despise the unsightly woman, and she brings forth a splendid little boy - Baganda proverb, Uganda

A child comes only as a gift from God - Ibo proverb, Nigeria

One is born, one is dies; the land increases - Oromo proverb, Ethiopia

Old habits die hard (it is very difficult to change an established pattern of behavior) - English proverb

A child is a source of blessings - Ibo proverb, Nigeria

When a lion gets old even flies attack him - Wadchagga proverb, Tanzania

He who laughs last, laughs best (the person who succeeds in making the last move has the most fun) – English & Somali proverbs

Look before you leap (consider all aspects of a situation before you take any action) - English & Somali proverbs

It is better to have no law than not enforcing it - Bantu proverb

The owner of the house knows where his roof leaks - Bornu proverb

Who wakes and rises at the first cry of the songbird collects the best fruit of the night, Beti proverb - Cameroon

A fool and his money are soon parted (a foolish person quickly spends his or her money on worthless things) - English proverb

The leopard's skin is beautiful, but his heart is evil - Baluba proverb

He who listens to the voice of the elderly is like a strong tree; he who turns a deaf ear is like a twig in the wind - Nilotic proverb

A lie can annihilate a thousand truths - Ashanti proverb, Ghana

Barking dogs seldom bite (people who threaten others usually do not hurt them) - English proverb

No matter how full the river is, it wants to swell further - Congolese proverb

Better a live coward than a dead hero (it's better to run from a life-threatening situation than to fight and risk being killed) - English proverb

During a storm you do not take shelter under just one roofing tile - Bayansi proverb, Democradic Republic of Congo

Only what you have combated for will last - Yoruba proverb, Nigeria

The apple doesn't fall far from the tree (children take after their parents) - English proverb

The wise are as rare as eagles that fly high in the sky - Bantu proverb

If you can't stand the heat, get out of the kitchen (if you can't tolerate the pressure of a particular situation, remove yourself from that situation) - English proverb

Working in the fields is hard, but hunger is harder - Nilotic proverb

Where the cattle do not graze, the warriors pass - Nilotic proverb

You cannot teach an old dog new tricks (elderly people can't change their behaviors or learn anything new) - English proverb

Leave well enough alone (don't try to improve something that is already satisfactory) - English proverb

Evil penetrates like a needle and then becomes like an oak tree - Ethiopian proverb and equivalent to Somali proverb which says "Baldness often starts abruptly (everything that you are not aware of comes suddenly, so it's necessary for one to be very careful by his/herself and to be cautious all the time in order to be safe and sound)"

The drums of war are the drums of hunger - South African proverb

The death of an elderly man is like a burning library - Ivorian proverb, Ivory Coast

A dog knows the places where he is thrown food - Acholi proverb, Uganda

If the tiger sits, do not think it is out of respect - Nilotic proverb
Once the mushroom has sprouted from the earth, there is no turning back - Luo proverb, Kenya

The hunter that speaks too much, goes home empty handed - Nilotic proverb

Hunger pushes the hippopotamus out of the water - Luo proverb, Kenya

A child's lie is like a dead fish in a pond that in the end always comes to the surface (explains his mother) - Luo proverb, Kenya

If the metal is not good, you cannot take it out on the blacksmith - Ekonda proverb, Democradic Republic of Congo

The owner of the dog does not obey his dog - Pygmies proverb, Democradic Republic of Congo, Congo, Cameroon, Gabon, Central African Republic, Rwanda, Burundi & Uganda

If he is not lost, do not look for him - Baoul proverb

Asking questions is not silly - Swahili proverb

You can't have your cake and eat it too (you can't enjoy the advantages of two conflicting activities at one) - English proverb

Blood is not water - Swahili proverb

If you kill a little hippopotamus, you also kill his mother - Bangala proverb, Democratic Republic of Congo

Every stream has its source - Zulu proverb, South Africa

Every man leaves his footprints - Nilotic proverb

Equality is difficult, but superiority is painful - Serere proverb, Senegal

A sandstorm passes; the stars remain - Nilotic proverb

Do as I say, not as I do (follow my advice, but don't follow my examples) - English proverb

The injured animal is covered with flies - Nilotic proverb

A village without elderly is like a well without water - Nilotic proverb

A father without sons is like a bow without arrows - Nilotic proverb

Old and new millet seeds end up in the same mill - Acholi proverb, Uganda

Take my knowledge, but not my behaviors - Arab proverb

If you can't beat them, join them (if you can't defeat your opponents, join forces with them) - English proverb

A dog does not enter a home where they suffer from hunger - Mongo proverb, Democradic Republic of Congo

A nice day, a gift for a street peddler - Swahili proverb

If you do not seal the holes, you will have to rebuild the walls - Swahili proverb

Who mistrusts everybody is the real enemy of the village - Nilotic proverb

I have to learn how to walk on three legs when I am old, says the hyena - Bambara proverb, Mali, Niger

Passion and hatred are children of intoxicating beverages - Zande proverb, Sudan

The tail of the cow watches to the right and left - Wadchagga proverb, Tanzania
The heart of an evil person is never pure - Bamileke proverb, Cameroon and parts in Nigeria

You can lead a horse to water, but you can't make it drink (you can propose a course of action to someone, but you can't force that person to accept it) - English proverb

Who guards two termite hills returns empty handed - Bahaya proverb, Tanzania

It is easier to transport an ant hill than exercise authority in a village - Mongo proverb, Democradic Republic of Congo

The day never turns back again - Tupuri proverb, Cameroon

If you chase away an ant, all the ants will come and bite you - Pygmies proverb, Democradic Republic of Congo, Congo, Cameroon, Gabon, Central African Republic, Rwanda, Burundi & Uganda

An apple a day keeps the doctor away (eating an apple every day helps a person to stay healthy) - English proverb

A youth that does not cultivate friendship with the elderly is like a tree without roots - Ntomba proverb, Democradic Republic of Congo

The black cow also produces white milk - Mandingue proverb

Two is company, but three's a crowd (couples often enjoy their privacy and dislike having a third person around) - English proverb

The mouth of an elderly man is without teeth, but never without words of wisdom - African proverb (anonymous)

If you shake a dog, you shake his owner - Rwandan proverb

It is strange! The ox eats hay and the dog eats bread, while the donkey carries wine but drinks water (who works more receives less) - Galla proverb, Ethiopia

Stretch your legs the length of your bed - Swahili proverb

Too many chiefs, no enough Indians (too many people are giving orders, and not enough people are following orders) - English proverb

Fly's legs, like the tongue of critics, land on whatever they find - Duala proverb, Cameroon

The rich is never satisfied - Bayombe proverb

We work on the surface; the depths are a mystery - Bahaya proverb, Tanzania

One swallow does not a summer make (one piece of evidence is not enough to prove something) - English proverb

You cannot teach an old gorilla the road - Fang proverb; Equatorial Guinea

The voyager's path is marked by the stars and not the sand dunes - Nilotic proverb

The best blessing for a good harvest is a pumpkin full of sweat - Mina proverb, Togo

Only the feet of the voyager know the path - Nilotic proverb

Harsh words hurt more than a poisonous arrow - Nilotic proverb

Who tells the truth is never wrong - Swahili proverb

Money does not grow on trees (money is not easily obtained) - English proverb

You cannot hide the smoke of the hut you set on fire - Burundian proverb

You do not teach a giraffe to run - Bantu proverb

A pilgrim, even if a sultan, is poor - Nilotic proverb

Man does not live by bread alone (people's psychological needs as well as their physical needs must be satisfied if they are to live) - English proverb

A monkey cannot dare what an elephant can - Duala proverb, Cameroon

Too many cooks spoil the broth (too many people trying to take care of something can ruin it) - English proverb

Two heads are better than one (two people working together can solve a problem quicker and better than a person working alone) - English proverb

The thorn will come out from where it went in - Bamileke proverb, Cameroon and parts in Nigeria

A friend is like a source of water during a long voyage - Nilotic proverb

A leopard cannot change his spots (a person cannot change his or her basic character once it has been formed) - English proverb

If you have a lot, give some of your possessions; if you have little; give some of your heart - Nilotic proverb

A mother's tenderness for her children is as discreet as the dwe that kisses the earth - Nilotic proverb
A friend works in the light of the sun, an enemy in the dark - Nilotic proverb

Rome was not built in a day (important things do not happen overnight) - English proverb

A united family eats from the same plate - Kiganda proverb, Democradic Republic of Congo

Between brothers, whether the trial is won or lost, makes no difference, Ekonda proverb, Democradic Republic of Congo

God provides for the blind vulture - Bambara proverb, Mali, Niger

No matter how early one awakes, the sun does not raise first - Nilotic proverb

The hunter knows his prey -Nilotic proverb

Practice makes perfect (doing something many times improves one's skill at it) - English proverb

The mouth makes debts, but the arms pay - Ewe proverb, Togo

The river swells from the little streams - Bateke proverb, Congo

There is more wisdom in listening than in speaking - Nilotic proverb

Misery loves company (unhappy people often get satisfaction from having others share their misery) - English proverb

There is no place like home (a person is happiest with his or her family and friends) - English proverb

What the chief likes is not always what the youths like - Bamileke proverb, Cameroon and parts in Nigeria
A friend is someone you share the path with - Nilotic proverb

The pen is mightier than the sword (the writen word is more powerful than physical force) - English proverb

Until the snake is dead, do not drop the stick - Ivorian proverb, Ivory Coast

Only a mother can understand the suffering of a son - Arab proverb

Clothes do not make the man (a person should not be judged by the clothes he or she wears) - English proverb

The bull should be taken by the horns, a man at his word - Bantu proverb

A united family eats from the same plate - Kiganda proverb, Democradic Republic of Congo

Who does not choose dies of hunger - Arab proverb

Beggers can't be choosers (when a person has nothing, he or she must accept whatever help is offered) - English proverb

Little by little the bird builds its nest - Mossi proverb, Burkina Fasso

The words of the elderly are as sweet as honey, but if you do not listen they become as sour as bile - Arab proverb

Discord between the powerful is a fortune for the poor - Arab proverb

A knife does not fear thorns, a woman fears man - Mongo proverb, Democradic Republic of Congo

You are never too old to learn (a person can learn at any age) - English proverb

Youths are like waves of the sea, the elderly have strength instead of tide - Arab proverb

Youths talk first and then listen, the elderly listen and then talk - Nilotic proverb

Nothing ventured, nothing gained (you can't achieve anything if you don't try) - English proverb

Where there are poor, there are rich. But where there is justice, they are all brothers - Arab proverb

The wind does not break a tree that bends - Sukuma proverb, Tanzania

The squeaking wheel gets the oil (those who complain the loudest get the most attention) - English proverb

In the desert of life the wise travel by caravan, while the fool prefers to travel alone - Arab proverb

Who made the drum knows best what is inside - Burundian proverb

Man is like a palm on the beach; moving with the wind of life - Arab proverb

The jaws have nothing to chew if the feet do not walk - Bakusu proverb, Kenya

It takes to to Tango (when two people work as a team, they are both responsible for the team's successes and failures) - English proverb

Who digs the well should not be refused water - Swahili proverb
One is not born a warrior, you become one - Arab proverb

A friend is like a water source for a long journey - Nilotic proverb

A man is known by the company he keeps (a person is believed to be like the people with whom he or she spends time) - English proverb

The thoughts of the wise are like stars in the galaxy: never ending - North African

The men are the wool of the tribe, but the women are the ones who weave the pattern - Arab proverb

In unity there is strength (a group of people with the same goals can accomplish more than individuals can) - English proverb

Do not wait until tomorrow to hunt - Nilotic prover

Those who waste time only hurt themselves - North African proverb

Youths look at the future, the elderly at the past; our ancestors live in the present - Nilotic proverb

When a lion roars, he does not catch game - Acholi proverb, Uganda

Birds of feathers flock together (people of the same type seem to gather together) - English proverb

A guest is a gift, a thief a tragedy - Nilotic proverb

The wisdom of the elderly is like the sun, it illuminates the village and the great river - Nilotic proverb

No pain, no gain (nothing can be accomplished without effort) - English proverb
Who does not understand a look, cannot understand long explanations - Arab proverb

A rich man who does not know himself is worth less than a poor man who does - Burundian proverb

During the dry season it is better to befriend the owner of the pirogue - African proverb (its origin is unknown)

Necessity is the mother of invention (most inventions are created to solve a problem) - English proverb

The tears running down your face do not blind you - Togolese proverb

You can live without a brother but not without a friend - Arab proverb

The worm that gnaws on the bean is the one inside the bean - Congolese proverb

If at first you don't succeed, try, try again (preserve until you reach your goal) - English proverb

Loving someone that does not love you is like loving the rain that falls in the forest - Western African proverb

Love is like a rice plant; transplanted, it can grow elsewhere - Madagascan proverb, Madagascar

Walking in two is medicine - Macua proverb, Mozambique

A Quarter of an hour is worth more than a thousand gold coins - Chinese proverb

Alone a youth runs fast, with an elder slow, but together they go far - Luo proverb, Kenya

He who hesitates is lost (a person who doesn't act decisively is unlikely to succeed) - English proverb

Charity is a silent prayer - Arab proverb

A man's heart is not a sack open to all - Rwandan proverb

A mother is like a kernel, crushed by problems but strong enough to overcome them - Balari proverb

Do not put your head in front of your words - Tupuri proverb, Cameroon

An empty sack cannot stand, Mandingo proverb - Guinea

Forewarned is forearmed (being warned about something before it happens allows a person to prepare for it) - English proverb

The heart is not a knee, it does not bend - Peul proverb, Senegal, Mali, Burkina Fasso, Cameroon, Chad, Nigeria, Mauritania, Togo and Niger

When your beard appears, childhood disappears - Rwandan proverb

The same water never runs into the same river - Ethiopian proverb

An undecided man is the worst disaster of the village - Nilotic proverb

Where there is abundance, there is poverty - Palestinian proverb

Who has no past, has no future - Palestinian proverb

The first step is always the hardest (the most difficult part of accomplishing something is getting started) - English proverb

If you are injured by a thorn, you will be healed by a thorn - Toma proverb

A fire cannot be wrapped with paper - Chinese proverb

A fool is like a wanderer lost on a path - Luo proverb, Kenya

A friend is someone who walks by your side - Luo proverb, Kenya

Where there's smoke, there's fire (when there's evidence of a problem, there probably is a problem) - English proverb

A generous man must eat if he wants to continue to be one - Nilotic proverb

A trial between brothers has no winners or losers - Ekonda proverb, Democradic Republic of Congo

A wrong step by the leader is a warning for those following - Bayombe proverb

A village united in fraternity is prosperous - Bayaka proverb, Central African Rebuplic

A village without elderly is like a tree without roots - Nilotic proverb

The road to hell is paved with good intentions (good intentions don't always lead to good actions) - English proverb

A village without elderly is unhappy - Luo proverb, Kenya

An abundance of food at your neighbour's will not satisfy your hunger - Bayaka proverb, Central African Rebuplic

Authority is in generosity - Tumbuka proverb, Zambia, Malawi, Tanzania

Beating drums is fun, but also tiring - Bangala proverb, Democradic Republic of Congo

Do not grab your heel until the ant has bitten you - Ekonda proverb, Democradic Republic of Congo

A miss is as good as a mile (losing by a narrow margin is no different than losing by a wide margin) - English proverb

Drums are never beat without reason - Kiganda proverb, Democradic Republic of Congo

Eggs and metal should not be put in the same sack - Ewe proverb, Togo

Equality is not easy, but superiority is painful - Serere proverb, Senegal

Eyes watch but cannot take - Bahaya proverb, Tanzania

Don't put the cart before the horse (don't do things in the wrong order) - English proverb

Happiness is like a field you can harvest every season - Luo proverb, Kenya

Hearing is not seeing - Swahili proverb

Hunger makes the big fish come out of hiding in the great river - Niliotic proverb

If a father does not cultivate, the son does not inherit land - Ekonda proverb, Democradic Republic of Congo

If you educate a woman, you have educated a population - Kiganda proverb, Democradic Republic of Congo

Don't put off for tomorrow what you can do today (don't unnecessarily postpone doing something) - English proverb

If you really love something, your fate is in its hands - Tupuri proverb, Cameroon

If you want something, you must work for it - Tupuri proverb, Cameroon

If your corn field is far from your home, the birds will eat your corn - Pygmies proverb, Democradic Republic of Congo, Congo, Cameroon, Gabon, Central African Republic, Rwanda, Burundi & Uganda

Intelligence is a fruit picked in the nieghbour's garden - Batabwa proverb

Don't put all your eggs in one basket (don't risk losing everything at once) - English proverb

It is better to be kind to our neighbors than to cross the world to offer incense to our ancestors - Unknown

It is easier to transport a termite hill than have authority in a village - Duala proverb, Cameroon

It is easy to pull a thorn out of someone else's skin - Burundian proverb

Once the manioca is in your stomach it's gone - Nyang proverb

One should not beg with a basket - Duala proverb, Cameroon

Don't look a gift horse in the mouth (don't complain about something that is given to you) - English proverb

One speaks badly of the absent but fears the present - Lula proverb
Only God generates, man only educates - Rwandan proverb

Don't judge a man until you'he walked in his boots (don't criticize a person until you'he tried to do the things he or she does) - English proverb

Rumours generate misunderstandings - Libinza proverb, Democradic Republic of Congo

Study without reflection is a waste of time, reflection without study is dangerous - Chinese proverb

The bird has no nest, but a branch to rest on - Bangwana proverb, Cameroon

The chicken that digs for food will not sleep hungry - Bayombe proverb

The chief's wisdom is a mesh of old stories, good and bad - Luo proverb, Kenya

The dog never forgets its owner, Bangala proverb - Democradic Republic of Congo

The earth is not an inheritance of our fathers, nor one for our sons - Luo proverb, Kenya

The frog does not tire in the water - Ngandi proverb

The heart is a locket that does not open easily - Duala proverb, Cameroon

The heart is not a knee, it does not bend - Peul proverb, Senegal, Mali, Burkina Fasso, Cameroon, Chad, Nigeria, Mauritania, Togo and Niger

The laziness of youths is worse than war - Tupuri proverb, Cameroon

The leopard does not eat fish (explanation: the chief does not handle irrelevant problems) - Ekonda proverb, Democradic Republic of Congo

Money is like the waters of a swelling river, it flows away - Ga proverb, Ghana

The monkey is a thief because it does not work - Tupuri proverb, Cameroon

The mouse says: I dig a hole without a hoe; the snake says: I climb a tree without arms - Basonge proverb

The predator lands on an unknown tree - Duala proverb, Cameroon

The river swells with the contribution of the small streams - Bateke proverb, Congo

The sore is cured but the scar remains - Ekonda proverb, Democradic Republic of Congo

The venemous snake cannot be seen in the Savannah - Niliotic proverb

The wind effects leaves, while violence men - Ovimbundu proverb, Angola

The wise man never takes a step too long for his leg - Egyptian proverb

The youth walks faster than the elderly but the elderly knows the road - Nilotic proverb

Those who sacrifice their conscience to ambition burn a painting to obtain ashes - Chinese proverb

Those who do not listen to the voice of the elderly are like trees without roots - Luo proverb, Kenya

To start a fight, one does not bring a knife that cuts but a needle that sews - Bahumbu proverb

The turtle does not suffer when running - Luo proverb, Kenya

War has no eyes - Swahili proverb

Wearing a mended dress is better than being naked - Unknown

What is hanging up, cannot be reached sitting down - Amhara proverb, Ethiopia

What the people think cannot be denied - Basakata proverb

What appears beautiful is not always good for you - Chinese proverb

When in someone else's home leave your defects at the door - Rwandan proverb

Where a river flows, there is abundance - Nilotic proverb

When the leg does not walk, the stomach does not eat - Nongo proverb

When you eat an egg do not insult the chicken - Bantandu proverb

When you need to make an important decision, never do it alone, choose the right people - Basakata proverb

When your neighbour is wrong you point a finger, but when you are wrong you hide - Ekonda proverb, Democradic Republic of Congo

Where there is a hippopotamus, be careful when passing with a pirogue - Nilotic proverb

Who created thunder does not fear it - Bahunde proverb

Who does not know the path should ask - Nilotic proverb

Who eats too much, will then be sick - Batabwa proverb

Who has shoes does not fear thorns - Ewe proverb, Togo

Who gets lost in the forest takes it out on who leads him back to the right road - Ekonda proverb, Democradic Republic of Congo

Who takes a hut, also takes the rats and cockroaches - Ntomba proverb

Who walks in the mud, at some point must clean his feet - Bahumbu proverb

Words can kill before arms - Nilotic proverb

You cannot hear a baby cry in the mother's womb - Bamfinu proverb

You are not born a leader; you become one - Bamileke proverb, Cameroon and parts in Nigeria

You can hide a mark on your skin, but not a defect - Burundian proverb

You can see the source of a river, but not that of a clan - Bayansi proverb

You do not beat a drum with one finger - Luo proverb, Kenya

You do not run into mountains, but people yes - Herero proverb, Namibia

You learn how to cut down trees cutting them down - Bateke proverb, Congo

You only understand the joys of parenthood when you have your first child; you only understand the mystery of death when in mourning - Bahaya proverb, Tanzania

You take a bull by the horns and a man by his words - Bantu proverb

You think of water when the well is empty - Ethiopian proverb

The mouth does not eat if the feet do not walk and the hands work - Bakusu proverb, Kenya

To form a dog is the ruin of education - Ekonda proverb, Democradic Republic of Congo

In the great river there are large and small fish - Ewe proverb, Togo

Who owns too much, remains unhappy - Tupuri proverb, Cameroon

The cultivator is alone, but those who eat are many - Schambala proverb, Tanzania

The leopard does not sleep on a dry branch - Pygmies proverb, Democradic Republic of Congo, Congo, Cameroon, Gabon, Central African Republic, Rwanda, Burundi & Uganda

A real family eats the same cornmeal - Bayombe proverb

The day does not return - Tupuri proverb, Cameroon

A puppy must not confront a large animal - Beti proverb, Cameroon

If you carry the egg basket do not dance - Ambede proverb, Gabon and Congo

Where the rooster crows there is a village - Schambala proverb, Tanzania

Before killing the chicken carefully observe the character of your guest - Mandingo proverb, Guinea

One rind is enough to tie a thousand pieces of wood - Amhara proverb, Ethiopia

If you want to lean on a tree, first make sure it can hold you - Ambede proverb, Gabon and Congo

One piece of green wood is enough to stop the others from burning - Bahaya proverb, Tanzania

Who follows the elephant will have no problems - Fante proverb, Ghana

If your cornfield is far from your house, the birds will eat your corn - Pygmies proverb, Democradic Republic of Congo, Congo, Cameroon, Gabon, Central African Republic, Rwanda, Burundi & Uganda

Money can even corrupt the virtuous - Vietnamese proverb

Only a fool believes that the clouds obscure the splendour of the moon. It has shined behind them for eternity – Unknown

The wind does not break a tree that can bend - Sukuma proverb, Tanzania

The elephant dies, but his tusks remain - Bamfinu proverb

Only the owner can free his home from mice - Bantandu proverb

Even your dog knows the homes of your friends - Batetela proverb, Democratic Republic of Congo

If the rhythm of the drum beat changes, the dance step must adapt - Kossi proverb, Burkina Fasso, West Africa

A stolen object does not fill ones heart with joy - Mongo proverb, Democratic Republic of Congo

No one knows if a bird in flight has an egg in its stomach - Dogon proverb, Mali and Burkina Fasso

Those who get on the same pirogue, have the same aspirations - Wolof proverb, Senegal, Gambia and Mauritania

Those who arrive to the spring first, drink the purest water - Sukuma proverb, Tanzania

Don't cry over spilt milk (don't grieve about having done something that cannot be undone) - Unknown

To guess is cheap, to guess wrong is expensive - Chinese proverb

The thread follows the needle - Batela proverb, Democratic Republic of Congo

Milestone cornmeal unites families - Tupuri proverb, Cameroon

The wind helps those without an axe to cut wood - Bamileke proverb, Cameroon and some parts of Nigeria

The moon lightens well but leaves certain areas in the dark - Vai proverb, Liberia

Though the leopard is fierce, it does not devour its cubs - Bantandu proverb

A raindrop does not spare the head of the notable - Beti proverb, Cameroon

A son will be what he was taught - Swahili proverb, East, Central and South Africa

Even the small leopard is called leopard - Bambala proverb, Ethiopia and Kenya

Sweet and sour walk hand in hand - Efik proverb, Nigeria

We rest our legs, but never our mouths - Bahaya proverb, Tanzania

The strength of the elderly is in the ears and on the lips - Mossi proverb, Togo, Burkina Fasso and Mali

A long voyage begins with just one step - Philippinian proverb, Philippine

It is easier to cover our feet with sandals than to cover the earth with carpets - Indian proverb

The toad that wanted to avoid the rain fell in the water - Bayansi proverb, Democratic Republic of Congo

Do not insult a crocodile while your feet are still in the water - Nilotic proverb

Even if thin, the elephant remains the king of the forest - Duala proverb, Cameroon

If the needle doesn't pass, the thread doesn't follow - Ambede proverb, Gabon and Congo

If a bird does not recognise a tree, it will not rest on it - Duala proverb, Cameroon

A small axe is not sufficient to cut down a large tree - Mongo proverb, Democratic Republic of Congo

Do not throw away the oars before the boat reaches the shore - Mpongue proverb

The womb is not a boat; it cannot carry as much - Duala proverb, Cameroon

Even without drumbeats, banana leaves dance – Ekonda Proverb, Democratic Republic of Congo

If a frog leaves the swamp for the mountains, it means it is in danger - Bantandu proverb

The sun shines during the day, not at night - Mongo proverb, Democratic Republic of Congo

A turtle never abandons its carriage - Basuto proverb, South Africa

The hand assists the foot, but the foot cannot do the same - Mongo proverb, Democratic Republic of Congo

An egg today is better than a chicken tomorrow - Vietnamese proverb

Clothes should not be made for an unborn child - Bangala proverb, Democratic Republic of Congo

After the storm the sun comes out - Vietnamese proverb

You cannot think you could teach a fish to swim - Asian proverb (its origin is unknown)

The corpse of a bird does not decompose in flight, but on the ground - Duala proverb, Cameroon

You are invited to join the hunt when your nets are in evidence - Ntomba proverb, Democratic Republic of Congo

A genius is he who is first to be right - Duala proverb, Cameroon

An elephant grows and becomes an adult, even if people do not like it - Vai proverb, Liberia and Sierra Leone

The mouth does not forget what it tasted only one time - Bahaya proverb, Tanzania

When a tree is cut down, a child can climb it - Vietnamese proverb

When there is will, there is a solution (hope) - Vietnamese proverb

The path leads towards loved ones not thorns - Duala proverb, Cameroon

Without effort no harvest will be abundant - Burundian proverb, Burundi

A knife does not recognise its owner - Mongo proverb, Democratic Republic of Congo

The new moon cannot come until the other has gone - Bahunde proverb, Democratic Republic of Congo

If you want to clear the land secretly, the noise of the axe will give you away, Ekonda proverb - Democratic Republic of Congo

Though it is the hand that gives, the man must be thanked - Basonge proverb

A hammer does not work with iron, Mongo proverb - Democratic Republic of the Congo

A friend when in need is a faithful friend - Vietnamese proverb

The buffalo does not wander from the marsh where it was born - Ngbaka proverb, Democratic Republic of the Congo, Central African Republic

Roots do not know what a leaf has in mind - Mongo proverb, Democratic Republic of Congo

Until the old moon disappears completely, the new moon can not come - Chinese proverb

A camel does not tease another camel about his humps - Egyptian proverb

Pretend you are dead and you will see who really loves you - Bamoun proverb, Cameroon

A goat never grazes in the same place - Duala proverb, Cameroon

Eggs should never be beaten with stones - Sao Tome & Principe proverb, West Africa

Beautiful day, a gift for the traveler - Indonesian proverb

Wisdom can be found traveling - Sri Lankan proverb

Confiding a secret to an unworthy person is like carrying grain in a bag with a hole - Nilotic proverb, African

If you are patient in a moment of anger, you will spare yourself one hundred days of tears - Cambodian proverb
There is no evil without goodness - Costarican proverb, Central America

The larger the ship, the larger the storm - Argentinian proverb, Argentine

A book is like a garden in the pocket - Indian proverb

Envy for a friend is like the taste of a sour pumpkin - Peruvian proverb, Peru

Where there are trees there are no builders - Mexican proverb

A stolen object brings no joy to one's heart - Uruguayan proverb, Uruguay

When a mother has twins she must sleep on her back - Peul proverb, Senegal, Mali, Burkina Faso, Cameroun, Chad, Nigeria, Mauritania, Benin, Togo, and Niger

Even if a baby seems unpleasant to look at, his mother never refuses him - Bamoun proverb, Cameroom

Time and tide wait for no man - Chinese proverb

If the well is distant, its water does not quench the thirst of the pilgrim - Chinese proverb

You cannot be a mouse and a bat at the same time - Beti proverb, Cameroon

Who does not love to dance, does not love to sing - Lango proverb, Lango is the name for two distinct languages spoken in Sudan and Uganda

Strong souls have willpower, weak ones only desires - Chinese proverb

Necessity is mother of every invention - Mexican proverb

Death is like a dress that, at some point or another, everyone has to wear - Mandingo proverb, Gambia, Guinea Bissau, Liberia, Senegal and Sierra Leone

There is no better mirror than a best friend - Cape Verde proverb, West Africa

Not even the five fingers of our hands are alike - Afghan proverb
Donated vinegar is sweeter than honey - Afghan proverb

When weeds invade the land, it means the owner is absent - Bahumbu proverb. Humbu is a dialect of Lunda, spoken in Zambia & East Africa

Those who seek revenge must remember to dig two graves - Chinese proverb

A rooster does not sing on two roofs - Ntomba proverb, Democratic Republic of Congo

A baby cannot be heard crying in his mother's womb - Bamfinu proverb, Democratic Republic of Congo

Only when a tree has grown can you tie your cow to it - Jabo proverb, Liberia

The skin of the leopard is beautiful, but not his heart - Baluba proverb, (Luba-Kasai) Democratic Republic of Congo

A wise man is able to adapt to the surprises of life as water to the decanter it is poured in – Chinese proverb

Deat is like a robe everyone has to wear - Mandingo proverb, Guinea and is equivalent to Somali proverb which says "Death and justice affect all men equally"

Between imitation and envy, imitation is better - Ekonda proverb, Democratic Republic of Congo

Don't judge a book by its cover (don't form an opinion about something based on appearance alone) - English proverb

The house of the heart is never full – English proverb

Don't open a shop unless you like to smile – Chinese Proverb

Appendix I

The Beautiful Names 'attributes' of Allah

The Name	The Meaning
Alaakhir	the Last
Alawal	the First
Albaacith	the Resurrector
Albaadi'	the Originator
Albaadin	the Hidden
Albaaqi	the Everlasting
Albaari	the Orderer
Albaarri	the Doer of Good
Albaasit	the Reliever
Albasiir	the Seer
Alcaadil	the Just
Alcaalii	the Highest
Alcadiim	the Great
Alcafuwa	the forgiver
Alcaliim	the Knower
Alcaziiz	the Precious
Aldaar	the Creator of Harm
Alfataax	the Opener
Alhaadii	the Guide
Aljaamic	the Gatherer
Aljabbaar	the Courageous
Aljaliil	the Mighty
Alkabiir	the Greatest
Alkariim	the Generous
Alkhaafid	the Restrictor
Alkhaaliq	the Creator
Alkhabiir	the Aware
Allatiif	the Gentle
Almaajid	the Majestic
Almaalik	the King
Almaanic	the Preventer of Harm

Almajiid	the Glorious
Almatiin	the Forceful
Almu'akhir	the Delayer
Almu'iz	the Honorer
Almu'min	the Inspirer
Almubdic	the Originator
Almuciid	the Restorer
Almudhil	the Subduer
Almuhaymin	the Guardian
Almujiib	the Responder
Almumiit	the Taker of Life
Almuntaqim	the Avenger
Almuqadim	the Expediter
Almuqiit	the Nourisher
Almuqnii	the Enricher
Almuqsid	the Equitable
Almuqtadir	the Creator of Power
Almusawir	the Shaper
Almutacaali	the Supreme
Almutakabbir	the Greatest
Almuxsin	the Appropriator
Almuxyi	the Nourisher
Alnaafic	the Beneficent
Alnuur	the Light
Alqaabid	the Holder
Alqaadir	the Able, Powerful
Alqafaar	the Forgiving
Alqafuur	the Forgiver
Alqahaar	the Conqueror, Subduer
Alqani	the Rich, the Self Sufficient
Alqawi	the Strong
Alqayuum	the Eternal
Alquduus	the Pure and Holy
Alra'uuf	the Kind
Alraafi	the Raiser
Alraqiib	the Watchful
Alrashiid	the Righteous
Alraxiim	the Merciful

Alraxmaan	the Compassionate
Alrazaaq	the Sustainer
Alsabuur	the Patient
Alsalaam	the Savior
Alsamad	the Eternal
Alsamiic	the Hearer
Alshaahid	the Witness
Alshakuur	the Rewarder
Altawaab	the Guide to repentance
Alwaajid	the Finder
Alwaali	the Governor
Alwaarith	the Inheritor
Alwaasic	the Magnanimous
Alwaaxid	the Only One
Alwaduud	the Loving
Alwahaab	the Giver
Alwakiil	the Trustee
Alweliyu	the Protector
Alxaafid	the Preserver
Alxaamid	the Praised
Alxakiim	the Judge
Alxakiim	the Wise
Alxaliim	the Gentle
Alxaq	the Truth
Alxasiib	the Accounter
Alxayi	the Living
Alzaahir	the Manifest
Duljalaal	the Lord of Majesty
Maliku-al-mulki	the Owner of All
Wal-Ikraam	the Bounty

Appendix II

Prophet Muhammad's Names and Descriptions
(Peace be Upon Him)

The Name	The Meaning
Amiir	Commander, Orderer
Axmad	Commendable, Praiseworthy
Bashiir	Forerunner, Precurser
Caadil	Just, Right
Caaqib	End, Termination
Cabdullaahi	the Servant of Allah
Daaci	Caller
Dayib	Good, Chaste
Faatix	Opener, Conqueror
Haad	Guide, Leader
Jawaad	Generous, Bountiful
Khaatim	Last of, Seal
Maah	Worn-out, Threadbare
Maamuun	Trustworthy, Safe
Macluum	Known, Famous
Mansuur	Victorious, Triumphant
Mash-huud	Attested, Proven
Matiin	Hard-wearing, Solid
Mahdi	Leader, Guide
Mubbashir	Preacher, Evangelist
Mubiin	Evident, Clear
Muhammad	One Worthy of Praise
Maxamuud	Praiseworthy
Mujtabba	Selected, Chosen
Muxarram	Forbidden, Sacred, Honored, Noble
Munaaj	Saviour, Rescuer
Muniir	Luminous, Brilliant
Masaddiq	Credible, Believable
Muddahir	Purifier, Clarifier

Muddeec	Obedient, Willing
Muqtasid	Wise, Intelligent
Murtadha	Chosen, Agreeable
Mustafa	Chosen, Selected
Muzakir	Reminder, Reminiscent
Naah	Prohibiter, Prohibitor
Nebbi	Prophet, Seer
Najii-Ullah	Confident of Allah
Naziir	Forerunner, One
Qariib	Near, Close
Rasuul	Messenger, Courier
Saadiq	Truthful, Righteous
Safii-Ullah	Best Friend of Allah
Shaahid	Witness
Shaafi	Curative, Tending to Heal
Shahiid	Martyr, Deceased warrior
Shahiir	Well Known, Famous
Sayyid	Chief, Head, Boss
Siraaj	Night Lamp
Xaamid	Grateful, Praiseworthy
Xabiibullah	Beloved of Allah

Appendix III

Prophet Muhammad's Wives
(May Allah be pleased with them)

The wives of Prophet Muhammad (peace be upon him) were called, "Mothers of the Faithful" and they were:

The Name	The Meaning
Khadijah	Great
Sa'udah	Black
Aisha (Ayesha)	Living, prosperous
Hafsa	Young lioness, young cub
Zainab	Beautiful, aromatic tree
Um-Salamah	Mother of peace
Safiyah	Pure
Zainab Bint Khuwzayma	Beautiful, aromatic tree
Um-Habibah	Beloved mother
Maymuunah	Blessed
Maryum (Maria)	Pure
Juwayriyah	Neighbor

Appendix IV

Prophet Muhammad's Children

Prophet Muhammed married eleven wives but only two births children for him and they were:

Khadija Bintu Khuweylat begets six children and Umatul Khatbiyah for one child.
1. Qaasim who died in Makka when he was only two years old
2. Zainab married and births one child named Ali who died at age two and she died the eight year of the Hijra
3. Ruqiya married by Osman Bin Affan and births Abdullah who died at age of eight. Ruqiya died the eighth year of the Hijrah
4. Fatima married Ali Bin Abu Dalib and births three boys (Xasan, Xuseen & Muxsin) and three girls Zainab, Ummulkalthum and Ruqiya. Only Xasan & Xuseen had children others died in early young age
5. Ummulkalthum married by Cusmaan Bin Cafaan after her sister Ruqiya who was his first wife died. She died in the nineth year of the Hijrah withour bearing any children.
6. Cabbdullaahi also known as Tahir or Tayib who died in early age too.
7. Ibraahim from Umatul Khatbiyah was the youngest of all and died when he was 22 months old in the eight year of the Hijrah.

Appendix V

Pre-faith (paganism) names in the Somali nomenclature system:

Before the coming of the Christian and Islam faiths in the horn of Africa, the Eastern Cushitic-speaking peoples had an ancient common religion, which is still professed by the Borana and among other minor peoples in the region. One of the most characteristic elements of that religion is connected with the notion of the *sky-God* called *Waaq*. Therefore, any name with the word *'Waaq'* in its composition is mentioning the *'sky-God'* and indicating that the name is used before the lunar faiths expanded to the region.

Also, it is worth to mentioning that today the word *'Waaq'* stands as the only God that Islam exercised and the word itself converted to Islam as people converted to that faith. Thus, Addoonwaaq could be translated as Cabdullah or the 'servant of Allah". Anyhow, all these names below as you will note have the word *'Waaq'* somewhere in the middle or the end and could be an enough example about the paganism era names in the Somali nomenclature system.

Addoonwaaq	sky God's servant
Shirwaaq	sky God's assembly
Amartiwaaq	result of sky God's superiority
Barwaaq	Sky God's niche or mark
Biddewaaq	sky God's servant
Caabudwaaq	sky God's worshiper
Ciqwaaq	sky God's sound
Dalwaaq	sky God's land
Diintiwaaq	Sky God's faith
Doorwaaq	sky God's choice
Guddoonwaaq	sky God's verdict
Naxariiswaaq	sky God's mercy
Siinwaaq	sky God's gift

Sunwaaq	sky God's poison
Tagaalwaaq	sky God's left-over or gift
Tagallewaaq	sky God's grace
Waaqdoor	sky God's choice
Waaqmahadle	thanks to sky God
Warwaaq	sky God's news
Warwaaqsame	sky God's good news
Jidwaaq	sky God's way
Ceelwaaq	sky God's well or waterhole
Xusuuswaaq	sky God's memory
Xorwaaq	sky God's edge
Xiinwaaq	sky God's hiss or speed
Sugaalwaaq	sky God's expectation
Seedwaaq	sky God's tendon
Sonkorwaaq	sky God's sugar
Nafwaaq	sky God's soul
Garashowaaq	sky God's wisdom or recognition
Guulwaaq	sky God's victory
Galladwaaq	sky God's favore or gratitude
Shanqarwaaq	sky God's noise
Lafwaaq	sky God's bone
Ducowaaq	sky God's invocation
Martiwaaq	sky God's guest
Miidwaaq	sky God's nectar or syrup
Warwaaqjecel	lover of sky God's word or news
Garwaaq	sky God's case or justice
Geelwaaq	sky God's camel
Doodwaaq	sky God's debate
Tiswaaq	sky God's drop
Roobwaaq	sky God's rain
Hawlwaaq	sky God's act
Hantiwaaq	sky God's property
Korwaaq	sky God's surface
Naruurowaaq	sky God's good action
Loxoswaaq	sky God's place or house
Liinwaaq	sky God's lemon
Saanwaaq	sky God's hide, footprint or sentry
Socotowaaq	sky God's travelers

Soofewaaq	sky God's whetstone
Sullanwaaq	sky God's descent
Hoorwaaq	sky God's raindrops or gush
Haatufwaaq	sky God's divine voice
Hilinwaaq	sky God's street
Garaadwaaq	sky God's judgement or mind
Horseedwaaq	sky God's vanguard
Hiyiwaaq	sky God's sense or center of emotion
Kolonwaaq	sky God's lappet or tassel
Kaswaaq	sky God's mind or intention
Lubbiwaaq	sky God's core, desire or heart
Haanwaaq	sky God's vessel
Hirwaaq	sky God's wave or surge
Yabarre	hypnotizer; exorcizer
Yabarcadde	proven; articulated hypnotizer
Yabarmadoobe	unproven; unarticulated hypnotizer
Yabarow	hypnotizer; exorcizer
Yeelwaaq	sky God's strap or leather cord
Dawowaaq	sky God's medicine
Sareedowaaq	sky God's good fortune
Sinjiwaaq	sky God's heridity
Hoobaanwaaq	sky God's ripe fruit
Wardoonwaaq	sky God's intelligence force
Hooswaaq	sky God's shadow
Turxaanwaaq	sky God's deformity
Guulle	giver of victory; God

Abbreviations

~	or
Arb	borrowed from Arabic
Cf:	confer with, please see (the cross-referenced word)
f	female
Lit:	literally means
m	male
Syn:	synonym (word with the same meaning)
i.e	example
etc	et cetera

A Note on the Author

The author, Anwar Maxamed Diiriye is a native of Somalia. He was born the Salamaca-dheer, a soft soiled grazing area southwest of Jiriiban district of the Mudug region, in approximately April 1968. He grew up partially in Gaalkacyo district and Lafoole of Afgooye district. He is a son from a broad nomadic traditional family and in his early childhood he was a herder of young sheep *'naylo'* and goats *'waxaro'*. Although he spent only first five years of his whole life as a nomad he still prefers traditional nomadism to pseudo-civilized urbanism, which uprooted the former. Mr. Diiriye is a Medical Laboratory Technologist by profession but he has a passion for history, culture, language and literature. He currently lives in Minneapolis, Minnesota, as an independent researcher. Mr. Diiriye is co-founder and the managing editor of Gobaad Socio-cultural and Literary Journal. He writes about social and health issues and he composes poetry in his spare time. Above all, Mr. Diiriye is a keen collector of both written and oral Somali materials.

Bibliography

Abd-el-Jawad, Hassan. 1986. *'A Linguistic and Socio-cultural Study of Personal Names in Jordan'*. Anthropological Linguistics, XXVIII
Abokor, Axmed Cali. 1987. *The Camel in Somali Oral Tradition Translated by. Xaange, Axmed Cartan.* Somali Academy of Sciences and Arts in Coorperation with Scandinavian Institute of African Studies, Uppsala
Achmed, Shire Jaamac. *Gabayo, Maahmaah iyo Sheekooyin Yaryar.* The National Printer's Ltd., Mogadishu
Afrax, Maxamed Daahir.1981. *Maanafaay.* Wakaaladda Madbacadda Qaranka. Muqdisho, Soomaaliya
--------. 1987. *Fan-Masraxeedka Soomaalida (Somali Theatrical Literature).* Kenya: Waxaa Fidiyey Allifaha (Distributed by The Author)
----------. *Rural Imagery In Contemporary Somali Urban Poetry: A Debilitating Carryover In Transitional Verbal Art.* School of Oriental and African Studies, University of London
--------. 1994. "The Mirror of Culture: Somali Dissolution Seen Through Oral Expression." Ahmed I. Samatar, *ed. The Somali Challenge: From Catasrophe to Renewal?* Boulder, CO: Lynn Reinner Publisher.
--------. 2003. *Ma dhabbbaa SoomaalidaDhaqankeedaa Burburka Baday?* Gobaad Cultural & Literary Paper, Minneapolis
--------. 2004. *Dal Dad Waayey & Duni Damiir Beeshay: Soomaaliya Dib Ma u Dhalan Doontaa?, (A Land Withoout Leaders in a World without Concience: Can Somalia be Resurrected?* London: Halabuur Communications
Al-Mubarakpuri, Safi-ur-Rahman. 1979. *Ar-Raheeq Al-Makhtuum (The Sealed Nectar): Biography of the Noble Prophet* (Peace be Upon Him). Islamic University Al-Madina Al-Munawwara.
Andrzejewski, B.W. 1964. *The Declensions of Somali Nouns.* London: University of London, School of Oriental and African Studies
Andrzejewski, B. W & Galaal, M. H. I., 1967. A Somali Poetic Combat, Michigan State University.
Andrzejewski, B.W., and Lewis, I.M., 1964. *Somali Poetry: An Introduction.* Oxford: At The Clarendon Press

Andrzejewski, B.W., and Sheila. 1993. *An Anthology of Somali Poetry.* Bloomington and Indianapolis, Indiana University Press

Armstrong, Karen. 1996. *Jerusalem: One City, Three Faiths.* Ballantine Books, New York

Ashby, Muata Abhaya. 1994. *Temt Tchaas: Ancient Egyptian Proverbs, Mystical Wisdom Teachings and Meditation,* edited by Asha. Miami, Florida.

Axmad, Axmad Sheekh Cali (Buraale). 1977. *Xeerkii Soomaalidii Hore.* Akadeemiyaha Dhaqanka, Muqdisho.

Bhabha, Homi K., ed.1990. *Nation and Narration.* Routledge. London.

Cabdicasiis Xasan Yacquub. *Qur'aanka Kariimka & Tafsiirkiisa oo Af-Soomaali ah.* Riyadh, Saudi Arabia.

Cerulli, Enrico. 1959. *Les Noms Personnels En Somali.* Scritti vari Editi Ed Inediti, Vol. 2, Edited by Enrico Cerulli. Somalia.

Ciise, Aw-Jaamac Cumar. 1974. *Diiwaanka Gabayadii sayid Maxamed Cabdulle Xasan: Uruurintii Koowaad.* Wakaaladda Madbacadda Qaranka. Muqdisho.

Diiriye, Anwar Maxamed. *Ballan Adduun & Buun Qiyaame (A Worldly Promise & The Honk of The Last Day).* Unpublished Paper

--------. Magac & Muuqaal *(The Name and the Look).* Unpublished Paper

--------. *Afka & Ummaddiisa (Language and Its People).* Unpublished Paper

E. Powys Mathers (Translator). 1986. *The Book of the Thousand Nights and One Night (Vol. 1) (Thousand Nights & One Night).* Routledge. London

Finnegan, Ruth. 1977. *Oral Poetry: Its Nature, Significances, and Social Context.* Cambridge University Press, London

Fowler, Alastiar. 1982. *Kinds of Literature: An Introduction to the Theory of Genres and Modes.* Cambridge, Harvard University Press.MA

Fraser, H. A & Brunner A., 1952. *Local and Scientific Names of the Fishes Collected on the Coast of the Trust Territory of Somalia*, Roma (F. A. O).

Galaal, Muusa Haaji Ismaa'iil. 1956. *Hikmad Soomaali* Edited with

Grammatical Introduction and Notes by B. W. Andrzejewski. Geoffrey Cumberlege, London.

--------. 1968. *The Terminology and Practice of Somali Weather Lore, Astronomy and Astrology.* Published By TheAuthor, Mogadishu

Hersi, Ali Abdirahman. 1977. *The Arab Factor in Somali History: The Origins and Development of Arab Enterprise and Cultural Influences in the Somali Peninsula.* Dissertation, University Of California Los Angeles

Kapchits, G. L. 1996. *Qaamuuska maamaahyada soomaaliyeed (The Dictionary of Somali Proverbs.* Vostochnaya Literatura, Russian Academy of Science. Moscow.

Kapteijns, Lidwien with Maryam Omar Ali. 1999. *Women's Voices In A Man's World (Women and the Pastoral Tradition in Northern Somali Orature, c. 1899-1980)* HEINEMANN, Portsmouth, N.H

Keenadiid, Yaasiin Cusmaan. 1976. *Qaamuuska Af-Soomaaliga (A Dictionary of the Somali Language).* Mogadisho

--------. 1984. *Ina Cabdille Xasan E La Sua Attivita Letteraria.* Istituto Universitario Orientale. Naples.

Keenadiid, Siciid Cismaan. 2005. *Soomaaliya: Maxaa Dheelliyey? 'Somalia: What is Out of Equilibrium?'* Amazon Printing Press, Sharjah, United Arab Emirates.

Johnson, John William. 1974. *Heellooy, Heelleelooy: The Development of the Genre Hello in Modern Somali Poetry.* Bloomington: Indiana University

Laitin, David D., 1977. *Politics, Language, and Thought: The Somali Experience.* University of Chicago Press.

Laurence, Margaret. 1963. *Prophet's Camel Bell.* McClelland & Stewart.

Laurence, Margaret. 1993. *Tree for Poverty.* ECW Press.

Lewis, I. M., 1961. A *Pastoral Democracy: A Study of Pastoralism And Politics Among the Northern Somali of the Horn of Africa.* International African Institute by the Oxford University Press. London, New York and Toronto

--------. 1998. *Peoples of the Horn of Africa: Somalis, Afar and Saho.* Haan Associates, London.

--------. 2002. *A Modern History of the Somali (Revised, Updated &*

Expanded). Ohio University Press; James Currey, Oxford; Btec Books, Hargeisa.

--------. 1959. *The Names of God in Northern Somali*, in "Bulletin of the School of Oriental and African Studies University of London" XXII, 1 London.

Manser, Martin H., 1992. *The Facts on Life Dictionary of Proverbs*. Facts on File, Inc

Maxamed, Maxamed Cabdi "Gaandi." Hal-abuur, Xirmo 01, Tr2 & 3, Dayr/Jiilaal 1993/1994. *Aafada Ummadda Soomaaliyeed Ku Habsatay Kadin Laga Baxo Ma Yeelan Kartaa?*

Maxamed, Maxamed Shire. 1974. *Maahmaaho Seddexshub ah.* Akadeemiyaha Dhaqanka, Muqdisho.

Mernissi, Fatima. 1993. *The Forgotten Queens of Islam*, Translated by Mary Jo Lakeland. University of Minnesota Press, Minneapolis

Mumin, Hassan Sheik. 1974. *Leopard Among the Women– Shabeelnaagood,Translated by* Andrzejewski, B.M., Oxford University Press.

Norrman, Ralf and John Haarberg. 1980. *Nature and Language: A Semiotic Study of Cucurbits in Literature*. Routledge and Kegan Paul. London.

Osman, Madina M. & Zorc, R. David. 1993. *Somali-English Dictionary with English Index*. Kensington, MA: Dunwoody Press.

Rirache, Mohamed Abdillahi. Somali Poetry: The Case of the Miniature Genres.

Royal Geographical Society. 1928. *First List of Names in Somaliland Protectorate.*

Samatar, Said S., 1982. *Oral Poetry and Somali Nationalism: The Case of Sayyid Mohammad Abdille Hassan*, Cambridge University Press.

--------. 1992. *In the Shadow of Conquest: Islam in Colonial Northeast Africa*. The Red Sea Press, Inc.

Samater, M. I., 11th Maggio 1967. *Proverbs as Cultural Vehicle*, in "Dalka" II, Muqdisho.

Sheik-Abdi, Abdi A. 1993. *Tales of Punt: Somali Folktales*. Published By Doctor Leisure, Macomb, Illinois

--------. 1994. *When a Hyena Laughs: A Somalian Novel.* Published

By Doctor Leisure, Macomb, Illinois

Sheniti, Mahmud. 1961. *'Treatment of Arabic Names'*, International Conference on cataloguing Principles Report.

Siddiqi, Muhammad Saeed, 1995. *The Blessed Women Of Islam*. Taj Company, New Delhi

Stevenson, Burton. 1948. *The Home Book of Proverbs, Maxims and Familiar Phrases*. New York, the Macmillan Company.

Stewart, Julia. 1996. *1001 African Names: First and Last Names From The African Continent*, A Citadel Press Book by Carol Publishing Group.

TheWorld Book, 2004. *The World Book Encyclopedia, 15th Volume.*World Book, Inc. a Scott Fetzer Company, Chicago

Titelman, Gregory Y., 1996. *Random House Dictionary: Popular Proverbs and Sayings*. New York, Toronto, London, Sydney And Auckland

Xaange, Axmed Cartan. 1984. *Dalkii Udgoonaa "The Land Of Spices"*. Muqdisho, Somalia

-------. 1988. *Sheekoxariirooyin Soomaaliyeed (Folktales from Somalia collected and translated by Ahmed Artan Hanghe*. Akadeemiyaha Cilmiga iyo Fanka Soomaaliyeed. Muqdishu, Soamaaliya; Colloborated with Scandinavian Institute of African Studies, Uppsala.

Zaborski, A., 1966-67. *Arabic Loan-words in Somali, Preliminary Survey*, in "Folia Orientalia" 8, Cracovia.

õõõ